Beautiful Agony

Jodi Lacroix

Published by: Restore for the Ages Press
ISBN: 979-8-9995524-0-2
Cover Design by Grace Dietz
Cover Photo: Wedding Reception, June 1986
Longmont, Colo.
Back Cover Photo by Tamas Kish
Layout Design by Elizabeth Petrucelli
Edited by Lisa Bourne

Beautiful Agony

A story of joy, grief, and hope

by Jodi Lacroix

Table of Contents

Joy

Grief

Hope

Conclusion

I dedicate this book to Our Lady of Fatima, my Heavenly Mother, and the kidnapper of my heart, who snatched me from my spiritual confusion, and led me to her Son. And to her Son, Our Dear Lord Jesus Christ, who is everything to me.

Miracle of the Sun, Oct. 13, 1917, Fatima, Portugal

Whenever I tell people that my husband fell out of our attic during a home improvement project, 25 feet down our stairwell, suffered paralysis and multiple injuries, lived inspirationally for almost a week in the hospital, and then died from a blood clot at the end of a successful surgery, their eyes grow wide, and they struggle for words. I'm sure that I wouldn't have known what to say to me either in that circumstance.

Yet the accident and loss of my husband John is only a tiny part of the beautiful agony of our lives. Here is our story.

Joy

John's Funny Pick-Up Line

Boulder, Colo., June 1983

In June of 1983 on a bright sunny day in Boulder, Colo., I was having the brakes on my Chevy Chevette fixed by two gentlemen friends, when someone special to both of us brought my future husband John Lacroix across the street to meet me. To use an old-fashioned word, there was an instant "spark" between John and me, possibly a "thunder-bolt." I saw the kindness of Jesus in John's eyes and in his smile. There is nothing more attractive about a man or woman than when you see the love of God shining out from inside them.

Being the owner of an orthodontic dental lab, John spoke to me the hilarious pick-up line, "Is that a lower retainer you are wearing?" And I fell for it, asking if he would like to see my retainer.

As we walked across the street towards his home to discuss dental things further, the two men working on my car were most likely wondering what had just happened. From that point on, for several months, nothing seemed to matter to us except getting to know each other better. It was "the beginning of a beautiful friendship," to quote a Humphrey Bogart line from the 1942 movie *Casablanca*.

John and I felt very comfortable in each other's presence, and we found that we had many things in common, including our Boulder hippy appearances. We talked, listened to music, and drank coffee for hours and hours together, basking in that giddy feeling of being totally distracted, not believing that someone like the other one existed. Our complete distraction when always thinking of the other was noticed by those around us. John and I were thrown for a loop in meeting each other. We feared each other at first.

We exploded into each other's hearts and into each other's lives, turning everything upside down and upsetting the apple cart of each of our futures. It was grand!

I had a commitment to leave for art school in Chicago in the fall, and John was under consideration for a dental lab manager job in Oregon. So, we lived large in the short time that we had left together and tried to make those moments really count, with drives in the mountains, cooking together and going to concerts.

Some background on John. He was born the second of five children in Toronto, Canada, in 1951, and shortly thereafter the family moved to Montreal. John's Dad Bruno was French Canadian, and his Mum Marguerite was German Scottish Canadian.

John's French genealogy traces back to the late 1690s in Quebec. English was spoken in the home, and according to John, he later learned French at the school bus stop to protect himself from getting beat up by his French speaking schoolmates. After High School John worked in his dad's jewelry store for a few years before attending Mount Allison University in New Brunswick. He took great joy in being a disc jockey on the radio at Mount Allison University in Sackville, New Brunswick, and at McGill University in Montreal, and in doing first responder volunteer work for the St. John Ambulance Brigade for three years.

After college John attained one of two available apprenticeships at Shaw Dental Laboratories in Toronto, beating out the other 2,000 applicants. He was trained in the dental technology field of orthodontics, and he brought those skills to the U. S. when he immigrated to Denver in August of 1978. John worked for many of the large dental labs in Denver before opening his own dental lab, Flatirons Dental Lab, in Boulder in 1981.

Some background on myself. I was born the second of two children in Indianapolis, Ind., in 1959, and six years later my family moved to Berea, Ohio, a suburb of Cleveland.

My Dad Bob was of English German descent, and my mom Harriet was of German Scottish descent. There are Mayflower and Revolutionary War ancestors in my genealogy, and I'm a member of the Daughters of the American Revolution (DAR).

My jobs during the school years included waitressing at various restaurants. Cleveland was a center for rock music, and I spent much time attending concerts. I attended Miami University of Ohio for one year, and graduated from Ohio University in Athens, Ohio with a degree in advertising from the School of Journalism in 1981.

After college I desired to explore the western part of the country, and I ended up in Boulder, Colo., in late 1981, working at various jobs and enjoying the Colorado lifestyle. Due to the economic recession of the early 1980's, I decided to develop my artistic skills by signing up for a two-year Commercial Art Associate degree program at the American Academy of Art in Chicago in 1983.

After leaving John in Colorado and upon arriving at my parents' home in Arlington Heights, Ill., for art school, I wavered in my decision to have a long-distance relationship with John.

The uncertainty of starting a new school, adapting to living with my folks again and knowing that I did not have my own self in good order, caused me to write a "Dear John" letter to my new love, and to be vague with him on the phone. I told John that while I certainly loved him, he deserved to be with someone very special, and that I just didn't have it together enough to be the right person for him.

This prompted John to write an amazing letter to me, letting me know that we were right for each other and that our relationship was worth fighting for. John told me that if we waited for everything to be in perfect order then we would fail. He sent a dozen red roses and a dozen yellow roses to me the day after his letter arrived.

My Dad answered the door, handed me the roses, and laughed.

Dad told me, "This one has your number!"

Which was probably true. All doubts about doing the hard work that a long-distance relationship entailed evaporated. I was all in. Wherever John was, that became "home" to me, and John felt the same way about me.

I've always appreciated that John was in favor of my attending art school in Chicago, even though we had just met and so wanted to be together. He did not want me to feel guilty for pursuing my dream, and he gathered up some of his art supplies to give to me. John wanted to know all about what I was learning the entire time I was in school, and he was totally supportive of my art school journey. Because John was so encouraging of my art school dream, I tried to be equally helpful with him in the pursuit of his dreams.

John soon visited Chicago to meet my parents. He had accepted a dental lab management job in Portland, Ore., and we made plans for me to visit him in Portland over Christmas break. John took me to Toronto, Ontario to meet his parents and family in early 1984.

We fought hard for our time together, spending many hours on the phone (at a time when long-distance calls were very expensive), writing letters (which we saved, and which I am now so thankful to have), and visiting each other during my school breaks.

For my birthday in May of 1984, John sent me a single song LP of "Hold On" by Minor Detail, an obscure Irish band of the early 1980s. The song lyrics were about holding on, being patient and waiting for each party to grow and mature in the ways necessary to be able to give the very best of themselves to the other. The song became our song together, and we worked to learn to love ourselves enough to be able to love others.

My time at art school gave me a chance to catch up with John in the maturity department and to properly prepare for our future together.

I worked a temporary job during my summer visit to Portland in 1984. We discussed a possible art school transfer to Portland for my second year, but we decided that my Chicago art school was superior.

So off I went to Chicago for another school year, and the letters, phone calls, visits, and the beautiful agony of being apart continued. One evening at the end of my second year in Chicago, John called me as the girl friend I was staying with went to bed. When she got up the next morning, John and I were still on the phone. She was amazed that we had anything at all left to say to each other.

Early in 1985 the dental lab John was managing in Portland was sold, and we decided that he would move back to Colorado and start up his own dental lab again. On February 1, 1985, John opened Mountain Vista Orthodontic Studio, and our lab has been in continuous operation until the present time. I graduated from school in June and moved back to Colorado as well. We were thrilled to finally be together in one state and began to discuss the prospect of marriage.

John always teased me about his proposal. One day I was discussing something with him, and I said, "And if we get married…"

He said, "Do you want to get married?"

I replied, "Are you asking me?"

He said, "Yes!"

And I said, "Yes!"

He then got up and called his mum in Toronto and told her that I had just asked him to marry me. I threw my shoes at him, and I could hear his mum laughing on the other end of the phone.

My dad's advice to me about marriage was to marry someone that you can go through the worst of times with, and the best of times with. And the best of times is more difficult because you tend to let your guard down and to quit working together as a team.

I didn't understand the accuracy of this advice until years later. I did take my dad's advice concerning John, as I felt that I could go through any situation with John. If we were together, we could seem to be able to face anything.

John had served as an altar boy in the late 1950s/early 1960s, and he loved the Latin Mass. He left the Catholic Church at the time of Vatican II in the 1960's, as he was not happy about the changes to the Mass.

John told me that he wished to marry me in the Catholic Church so that we would be married until death did us part. I agreed, and we began the Pre-Cana instruction at Immaculate Conception Church in Lafayette, between Boulder and Denver, with a very kind and patient priest. John and I scored very high on our compatibility tests, so there was hope for us to have a successful marriage despite all our faults and weaknesses.

God must have seen potential in us and for us, and the wedding was set to take place on June 21, 1986, three years to the day after we had met.

A Sunny Day in June

Immaculate Conception Church, Lafayette, Colo.,
June 21, 1986

We had very little money to get married with, and that did not matter to us. Our families helped us out as best they could.

I was a little late arriving to the wedding, as I had forgotten something and had to go back for it. When my dad saw me outside the church, he beamed at me and teared up. I felt the spiritual presence of my dad's parents there with us.

As my dad walked me up the aisle, I will never forget the grin on John's face. He smiled in a way that made me wonder if there was something he had forgotten to tell me, and I contemplated turning around and leaving. No, not really! Later John told me he was thinking of how much fun we were going to have. Very true!

The wedding was small. The approximately 40 guests were fabulous. The organist was found at the last minute, and she graciously blessed us with beautiful music. Our priest almost overheated after the wedding while posing for many pictures in his heavy cassock (full-length clerical coat). My brother was the photographer, Gospel reader, and rescuer of John's best man, whose car broke down on the way to the reception.

But the main thing that stood out for me was John's joy at coming back into the Catholic Church at our wedding Mass. He loved receiving Holy Communion, and John paused the wedding at the kiss of peace during the Mass to shake hands with everyone in the pews. I was truly happy for him.

Our reception at the Double Tree Inn in Longmont was lovely and fun. John's music selection impressed the disc jockey that we had hired from the radio station KBCO so much that he asked John for a taped copy to keep for himself. My art school friend from Australia had showed up the night before and graced us with her sunny personality and fabulous dancing skills.

John and I looked forward to dancing to our song, "Hold On," by Minor Detail, only to have my dad ask me to dance and my mom ask John to dance to the song. We smiled at each other while dancing with them and we felt blessed to have my parents there with us on that special day. While dancing together that evening, John and I told each other that if we stayed together, we could face anything in life that came our way.

Our wedding and reception brought us great joy, and during the years of our marriage we fondly reminisced about that day. We celebrated our anniversaries with great enthusiasm every year, and I kept an anniversary album for us replete with pages for 50 years. We figured that if we made it to our 50th anniversary, we could always cough up the money for some more pages.

Married Life

3 Margaritas Restaurant, Broomfield, Colo.,
October 2000

We began our married life with a pledge to try to always give 110% to our marriage, and to be completely faithful and honest with each other. John and I promised to never use the word "divorce" in any of our future disagreements, as this would lead to a break in our ability to trust each other.

The first big test of these goals took place for us while working in our dental lab together. We decided that we would work together, and that John would train me. It takes years to train someone to become a good dental technician. John was a good teacher, and an extremely tough boss.

Getting a chance to live the American Dream and own his own business made John very proud of our dental lab. He was a Certified Dental Technician, and for four years he was an Examiner in Dental Technology for the National Board for Certification, being skilled in all the areas of dental technology.

His standards were very high. He could be hyper critical at times. If he didn't like some of the wires I had bent for the retainers, or the way I polished the acrylic, he would have had no problem making me re-do the work, even if that meant more hours in the lab. We struggled sometimes to find the balance between who did what tasks, and what was the best use of our working time. It was never fun when I broke something, causing him to spend more time working on the repair. When I felt the short end of things, I would project the silent treatment, making things difficult for him.

Many people told us that they could never work with their spouses. We found that, despite the usual nattering and disagreements, if we began our workday with a fight, we ended the day in good spirits because we had to finish the work no matter what. And most of the time we couldn't remember what we had been fighting about anyway.

One of our favorite old TV commercials was the 1981 Dunkin' Donuts *"Time to Make the Donuts"* ad. The ad features a very tired looking man repeatedly walking out of his home while saying, "It's time to make the donuts!" He eventually meets himself coming in the front door, saying, "I already made the donuts!" John and I often used to look at each other in the early mornings and John would say, "It's time to make the retainers!" And I would say, "We already made the retainers a few hours ago!"

Marriage is extremely hard work, of course. We tried to focus on encouraging each other and always having each other's backs. Respecting each other's opinions and wishing the best for your spouse takes some practice. We talked about not worrying about the opinions of others and learning to trust each other completely. It's never easy to tell your spouse the hard truths they need to hear, but we worked on being painfully and hopefully charitably honest with each other when it was appropriate.

In most marriages, faults become clear to each other early on. We were no exception. There was door slamming, saying things we immediately regretted saying, walking out to cool off for a while, and trying to find a balance between what we wanted to do in our lives individually and together.

Learning to correct each other's faults in a charitable way takes work and patience, and most likely with eye rolling and sighing. Towards the later years of our marriage, we developed a contest for who could apologize to the other one first after a fight. We would sneer and grimace as we said, "I'm sorry," which made us laugh. Then we would fight over who said it first. And then laugh again.

John and I both liked to introduce each other to everyone, and we were comfortable with getting to know each other's friends. Speaking well of the other one and of our families was important to us. Many times, I remember walking into a room of many people and hearing John mentioning my name repeatedly in a positive way. He liked to brag about me, and I liked to talk about "my wonderful husband" with family, friends and strangers alike. I told many folks that, "I married well."

John loved to tease me, and he worked on finding an endless supply of ways to do that. Once I was telling him and a friend that according to the Church, there was no marriage in Heaven. Except I said there was, "no Heaven in marriage," thus giving John some teasing ammunition. He liked to teach me French phrases and mix another word into the phrase, setting me up to speak the phrase incorrectly. For instance, he taught me "Quelle fromage" (What a cheese!) instead of "Quelle dommage!" (What a shame!).

I had a "brown thumb" with plants, and whenever I attempted to buy a plant, he would ask me what that poor plant had ever done to be killed by me. John played the Marty Robbins song "El Paso" repeatedly, knowing that it drove me crazy, until I finally came to have a true appreciation for the story telling singer and songwriter, much to my consternation and to John's delight.

At Mass on Sunday mornings, John would lean over and say, "Don't think about breakfast" knowing that I was always hungry. When we once attended a very long Tenebrae service during Holy Week, I asked John if we could leave. He answered, "Could you not watch one hour with Me?" repeating what Jesus had said to the Apostles in the Garden of Olives.

On Saturday evenings, John would sometimes ask me if we needed to leave early for Church the next morning so that I could be sure to make it to Confession. And oh, how I loved it when he teased me!

John and I had a habit of talking on top of each other when we were telling stories to our friends, much to their delight. And we could both talk a blue streak.

John and I felt 110% alive when together, much like when we were teenagers and finding life always interesting, almost achieving that "childlike" joy of life. We were never bored, and whenever we heard someone claim they were bored, we wanted to ask them for their time, as we felt we didn't ever have enough time to do what we wanted to do. We had all kinds of inside jokes, sometimes seeming to speak our own language, and we began to finish each other's sentences.

John loved to tease my close girlfriends, never missing the opportunity to find something he could playfully bother them about. When I would go out with my girlfriends without him, he would advise me to put some "hinge wax" on the corners of my mouth so that I could talk faster.

We really missed each other during the rare times we were apart. If one of us was out of town, we would talk every day without fail. If I went back east to visit my mom, John would head for Home Depot and buy supplies for a weekend home improvement project. I would come home to find a newly remodeled bathroom or a newly installed window. It was almost scary when the workers would call out "Hi John" whenever we walked into Home Depot together.

A typical workday would begin with John rising at 4:30 a.m., running the coffee bean grinder, caffeinating up, and heading to Home Depot to browse the power tool aisle. He would come home, sit next to me on the bed and tell me of power tool sale items before I was fully awake. Sometime that afternoon in the dental lab he would remind me that I had given him permission to buy a power tool he found on sale, and I would protest.

I did encourage him to buy many power tools, as his home improvement skills were legion, and he saved us thousands of dollars with his many home projects and repairs. We loved doing these projects together, and we sometimes had to wait many years, even several decades, to be able to afford to make certain upgrades to our home.

John had a very quick wit and a great sense of humor. When checking out at Costco, the checker noticed that John had a dozen red roses and a large amount of toilet paper in his cart. He commented to John that it was an unusual order. John let him know that if he did not buy his roses for his wife, she would TP the house.

If I asked, "Do I look better now or when we got married?" he would answer, "You look wonderful at all ages."

Once when John came down with a powerful virus, he ended up requiring oxygen at night for a while. I soon came down with the same virus, so John put a tee in the oxygen tube, and we had "his and her" oxygen at night for a spell. He made me go outside the house to eat canned tuna because he couldn't stand the smell.

He liked to always see the silver lining to every situation, much to my consternation, or amusement, sometimes. He would say, "It was worth the thousands of dollars in repair bills to find out that we bought a lemon of a car. We'll know how to choose better next time."

John was a Grand Knight of his Knights of Columbus Council for several terms. He decided that as his wife I needed to be dubbed the "Grand Marnier," after the liqueur.

One day our sewage line backed up in our basement, and we found ourselves ankle-deep in sewage water. After a long saga of cleaning up and disinfecting, we were leaning against the washer and dryer and relaxing when we heard a gurgle, and then the sewage line backed up again. Standing in the ankle-deep sewage water for a second time, we looked at each other. John began to laugh, and soon we had tears streaming down our faces and we were engaging in a good belly laugh. We knew the grind ahead of us, but I was blessed to have a husband who helped me to see that it was okay to laugh right then, as it was an incredibly funny situation.

John developed a "hubby points" system, where he would do something extremely thoughtful for me, or he would offer the perfect romantic answer to a tricky question that I asked him, and he would then translate his reward into points. These "hubby points" were the numerical equivalent of dollars, and they usually amounted to the number needed to purchase a certain power tool or project supply. He was quick to run for the computer to hit the "Complete Purchase" button, so I had to be fast and careful in my responses.

In 2003, I required extensive jaw surgery. John asked our priests if he could be dispensed from Mass attendance so that he could stay at home with me for as long as necessary. After I was back in my hospital room following the surgery, the nurse came in and asked if John could come in to see me, as she said he was making a new pattern in the hallway tiles by pacing back and forth. He took beautiful care of me during my recovery, though it must have been quite disappointing to him that I was still able to talk right after my surgery.

When I discovered that I had many food allergies, John went on a special diet with me, and he made lots of efforts to help me find new ways to cook and to eat.

In 1991, we were asked to bury a statue of Our Lady that someone had vandalized at our parish in our yard. Instead of burying the statue, John put the hundred-plus pieces back together like a Chinese jigsaw puzzle and smoothed the cracks with automotive body filler.

Statue repair, Our Lady of Fatima, Lafayette, Colo., 1991

I repainted the statue, carefully matching the paint to the original colors. Our parish priest was amazed at the result, and from that year on, we restored and repainted Catholic statuary and other miscellaneous pieces of art in our off hours from the dental lab.

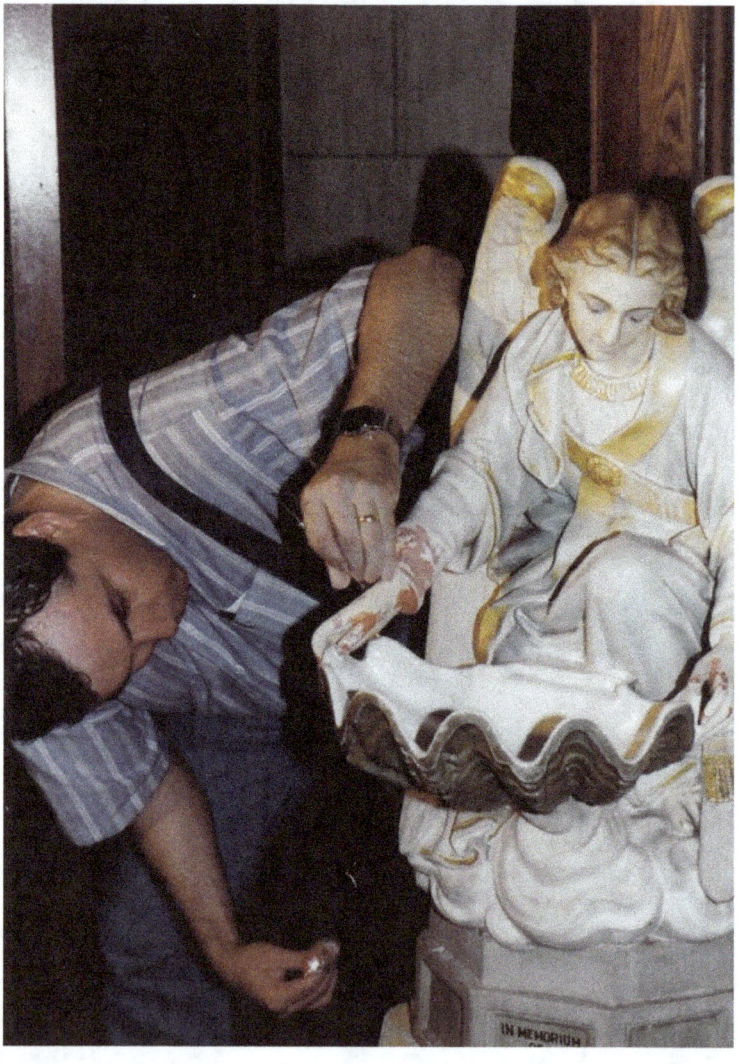

The projects grew larger throughout the years, and we were even asked to work on the underside of the famous "Spiral Staircase" in the Loretto Chapel in Santa Fe, N.M. in 1995. John re-plastered a large section underneath the stairs, and I re-painted and re-stained the area to make it look like wood. We also restored the "IHS" letters (a "Christogram", an ancient way of writing the word "Jesus Christ") on the Communion rail and several statues in the Loretto Chapel at that time.

Restoration work., Loretto Chapel, Santa Fe, N.M., May 1995

Restoration work, statue for Carmelite Monastery, Littleton, Colo., 2013

Restoration work for Sacred Heart Church Cemetery, Boulder, Colo., 2013

John fixed, re-stained, and re-sealed a large amount of our parish's pews in 2013. We restored and repainted a large pair of Daprato angel statues from the early 1900s for our parish church in 2013. John also repaired a cement statue in the Sacred Heart of Mary Cemetery in Boulder, Colo., and a statue of Our Lady for the Carmelite Monastery in Littleton, Colo.

If I was quilting, John went to the quilt store with me and helped me with fabric color selections. John attended many quilt shows with me, almost never appearing bored. If John was woodworking, I went to a woodworking show with him and watched demos and listened to the experts with him. I assisted him in the garage with many of his woodworking projects.

We were total art geek nerds in art museums, restaurants, and anywhere art was displayed. John had learned much from my art school days, and we would look at paintings and wax on about the color usage, composition, technique and perspective of the artist. Two of our favorite artists were William-Adolphe Bouguereau (1825–1905), a French realistic artist known for his beautiful Catholic figure paintings, and Jacques Joseph (James) Tissot (1836–1902), a French painter known for his extensive paintings of Jesus and Mary in the Holy Land. One Christmas John gave me the four-volume set of Tissot's "The Life of Our Lord Jesus Christ" from 1897, which contains many of Tissot's beautiful Holy Land paintings.

John worked in the restaurant at Jasper National Park in Alberta, Canada, one summer, learning the European wait staff rules. He was also a manager at several Denver restaurants. I worked at several restaurants and cafeterias during my Ohio school years. We both appreciated the hard work involved in owning, managing or working in the food service industry. We encouraged our kids to work at a restaurant for their first jobs, knowing that they would gain a lot of life experience from that type of job.

We were generous tippers, and we had many favorite mom-and-pop restaurants to frequent.

Some of our most loved places were George's Café and the Old Neighborhood Restaurant (both in Arvada, Colo.), Ting's Place in Lafayette, and Gussie's in Westminster, Colo. The owners and wait staff would often seat us at preferred tables, tell us jokes and talk about life with us. It pays to treat everyone in a restaurant well, and we knew about never making the waiters or cooks mad at us for anything, which is an inside restaurant joke about not knowing what happens to your food in the kitchen.

We contemplated opening a restaurant ourselves, but we realized that it would be extremely difficult to run a restaurant successfully long term. Some folks have a knack for making a restaurant prosper, and we loved to support their efforts with our patronage.

My description of John would be that he was a long-term thinking, consistent, frank, and honest man. He utilized the SOS strategy: stop, observe, strategize, in most matters of life. He was a true Catholic gentleman; a man whose great concern was usually to make everyone feel at their ease and at home. So many said of John in later years that "he was my favorite customer, client, patient, etc. Some who knew him said he was "genuine," "a straight shooter," and a man with solid common sense whose frankness was particularly useful when difficult decisions had to be made.

Our Spiritual Journey

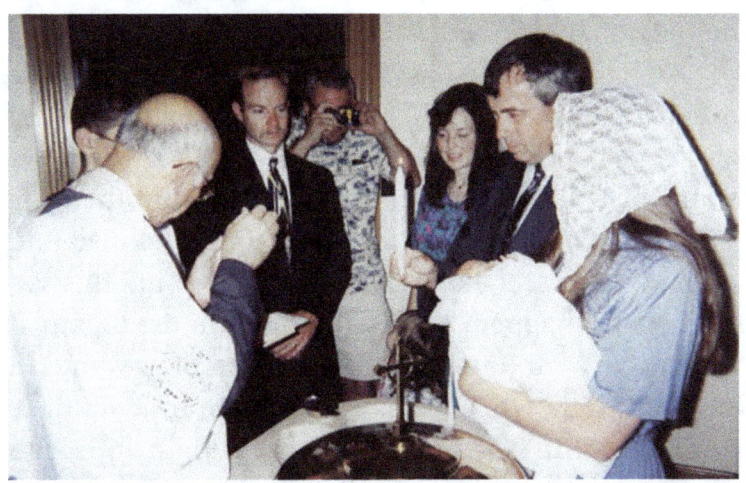

Baptism of our Goddaughter Colleen, Good Shepherd Church, Denver, Colo., June 2000

One day in the early 2000s, John drew concentric circles on a piece of paper. He pointed to the circle in the center and told me that God should be the center of our lives. The circle surrounding the center circle represented John and me and our family. Each circle further out represented our friends, acquaintances, etc.

He told me that this was the order we should strive to follow in our lives. By loving God more than each other, we would be able to love each other and others more abundantly in a way that we had never achieved before. This new order of putting God first became the secret to the success of our marriage and of our lives, despite the abundance of our flaws and shortcomings.

While discussing our hopes and dreams together, John drew up a chart listing all our family members, using different colored magic markers to define our short, medium, and long-term goals.

John and I discussed our deaths and final plans on several occasions. We had a good laugh talking about if the other spouse died early and would we want them to find someone else to live out their life with. The conversation turned serious when we told each other to seek happiness and love should this sad occurrence happen. We both wished to die together, perhaps in a car or plane crash. Neither of us wanted a sudden death, when there would be no time to make our peace with God and to put things right with Him when transitioning into the next world.

John frequently said, "It's all about Heaven." It was his response to any time when things were dicey, difficult, or problematic. I came to think of that phrase myself when things were tough.

I was raised in the Methodist and Presbyterian churches. I attended Catholic Mass with John after we were married. Two years later, someone told me the story of Our Lady of Fatima, where Mary, the Mother of Jesus, had appeared to three peasant children in a small village in Portugal.

What particularly piqued my interest was the Miracle of the Sun apparition, when approximately 75,000 people observed a miraculous solar phenomenon immediately after the Mary's final appearance to the children. I felt like Our Lady kidnapped me on that very day, as I suddenly began to notice her everywhere; on billboards, in songs on the radio, in magazines, and in artwork all around me.

At the same time, our pastor had realized I was not Catholic, and he instructed me to come to the rectory the next Monday morning, where he presented me with a copy of Father John Hardon's Catechism and offered to personally instruct me in the faith.

On a sunny Sunday in July of 1988, I received conditional Baptism, First Confession, First Communion, and Confirmation. John had not pressured me to convert to Catholicism in any way, and after my conversion he allowed me to buy any and all books about the Catholic faith. Soon it seemed that the weight of my book purchases almost made the foundation under our home library tilt to the west.

One of our favorite prayers was the Litany of Humility, written by Rafael Cardinal Merry del Val (1865–1930), Secretary of State for Pope Saint Pius X. We both recited the prayer daily, and John would say that he could only make glacial progress in the journey towards humility, even after reciting the prayer for several decades.

We attended Mass weekly, and more often if possible. John briefly taught CCD classes for teenagers preparing for the Sacrament of Confirmation, and I briefly taught CCD classes for young children preparing for First Holy Communion. John had taken part in the early pro-life marches in Ottawa, Canada in the 1970s, and we continued to work together in the pro-life movement in Colorado after we were married.

John was delighted to learn in the 1990s that a Latin Indult Mass was offered in Denver, meaning the parish had permission to offer it following reforms at the Second Vatican Council. John had a very strong attachment to the old form of the Mass due to his altar boy service in Quebec in the 1960s. So, in the late 1980s we attended the first Latin Mass at the Cathedral in Denver in four decades, and then occasionally attended the weekly Indult Mass at Good Shepherd Church.

In 1996, the traditionalist Priestly Fraternity of St. Peter (FSSP) sent a priest to Denver to offer the Latin Mass to the faithful there on a continual basis. John and I were among the first 16 or so people to attend the original Mass of Our Lady of Mount Carmel Latin Mass Community, which is now Our

Lady of Mount Carmel Church, a personal parish of the Archdiocese of Denver in Littleton under the spiritual and pastoral care of the FSSP.

John with Father Josef Bisig, Superior General of the FSSP, 1997 at Colorado Catholic Academy, Wheat Ridge, Colo.

Our Lady of Mount Carmel Church, 2001, Littleton, Colo.

Altar of Our Lady of Mount Carmel Church, 2001, Littleton, Colo.

At first, I was thoroughly confused with this form of Mass, having only known the Novus Ordo Mass, and I was constantly lost when trying to follow the prayers of the Mass. John suggested that I join the parish choir, as I love to sing. Learning to sing Gregorian Chant and Latin hymns really helped me to connect with the Mass, and I soon began to fall in love with all aspects of the Traditional Mass, especially the beautiful hymns and the chants of Holy Week and Christmas. Shortly after I joined the choir in 1996, I decided to play a joke on the other members. I inserted copies of "Kumbaya" with a fake hymn number in our binders. For years afterwards we would laugh about the hymn that didn't quite fit in with the traditional Catholic music we were singing.

We worked hard along with many others to build up the parish. Churches were rented for Christmas and Holy Week Masses. Our priests had a traveling mobile sacristy (where the priest prepares for Mass and where vestments and other sacred items used in the Mass are kept) in their cars. One Good Friday we had such an overflow at the school chapel that I was very concerned about the floor collapsing into the basement.

Cornerstone ceremony, Our Lady of Guadalupe Seminary, Oct.16, 1999, Denton, Neb.

In the late 1990s we learned that the FSSP would be building their new seminary, Our Lady of Guadalupe Seminary, in Denton, Neb. John and I were just about doing cartwheels when realizing that the seminary would be within driving distance for us. We attended the cornerstone ceremony in 1999. I can still see Bishop Fabian Bruskewitz, a larger-than-life figure, walking around the grounds of the seminary, his cope (full length vestment) flying behind him in the wind. We were told that the cornerstone of the seminary had been discarded by a construction company in Lincoln, Neb., so it was very fitting to have a seminary cornerstone that "the builders rejected."

SOLEMN BLESSING AND DEDICATION

OUR LADY OF GUADALUPE SEMINARY
DENTON, NEBRASKA

DECEMBER 9, 2000

Solemn Blessing, Our Lady of Guadalupe Seminary, Dec. 9, 2000, Denton, Neb.

The blessing of the seminary took place in 2000, and we attended Mass in the basement library room of the seminary. The seminarians had been up all night before, painting walls and taking care of last-minute details. The doorknob to the front door of the seminary had not yet been installed. It was glorious to see their extreme efforts to make the blessing ceremony so special. Every time John and I visited the seminary, we were treated like a visiting king and queen. I'll never forget the generosity and kindness of those young men towards us.

Consecration of Ss. Peter and Paul Chapel, Our Lady of Guadalupe Seminary, Mar. 10, 2010, Denton, Neb.

Consecration of Ss. Peter and Paul Chapel, Our Lady of Guadalupe Seminary, Mar. 10, 2010, Denton, Neb.

The dedication of the seminary's chapel in 2010 was one of the highlights of our lives. The Ss. Peter and Paul Chapel felt like a portal to heaven that day. The dedication of a seminary chapel is such a rare occurrence, and we were very honored to be there. Almost all the current priests of the FSSP at the time attended the dedication. Bishop Bruskewitz was quite tired after the all-day event, and he was still cheerful and willing to greet everyone at the day's end. Catholic network EWTN broadcasted the event globally.

We hosted Our Lady of Guadalupe seminarians many times when they visited our parish and Denver on their field trips. We had the FSSP priests and seminarians to dinner at our home, and John was the cook, of course! We always enjoyed their fine sense of humor and their ability to really enjoy life. We usually planned our vacations to cities where an FSSP apostolate church was available on whatever Sunday we were traveling.

In July of 2007 Pope Benedict XVI issued the apostolic letter Summorum Pontificum, which allowed all priests worldwide to be able to offer the Latin Mass if they chose to. Beforehand, priests were required to ask permission from their bishops to offer the Mass. Pope Benedict also named the Latin Mass the "Extraordinary Form" and the Novus Ordo Mass the "Ordinary Form." These steps helped those of us who regularly attended the Latin Mass to feel a much stronger sense of belonging to the Catholic Church.

We were given an abundance of joy in being asked to become godparents to several children in our parish. We also became "adoptive" godparents to many children and young adults in our parish, filling in as substitutes for those whose godparents were far away or who were maybe remiss in their spiritual duties.

We loved to discuss our dreams, our priorities, and our 'kingdom' together. Life became so much better when we put God above each other and everyone else.

I can remember John daily praying his Divine Office (his breviary, or book of daily prayers) in all different places in our home, our car, and in many other locations. It would take him about an hour each day. He had such a gentle sense of faith.

One Christmas Eve morning we were driving by some cows in a field. John told me that they had better rest up, as they had to be in an important manger scene that evening.

When I asked John what it was like to look into the eyes of our firstborn grandson, he said, "I saw eternity."

John's favorite Rosary mysteries were the Glorious Mysteries, and his favorite phrase of the Latin Mass was Sursum corda, which means, "Lift up your hearts."

At some point in our Latin Mass attendances together, John and I started to hold hands during the Last Gospel. It became a ritual, and we would be sure to hold hands at that point, even if we were at the back of the church getting ready to leave Mass ahead of everyone to work at a pancake breakfast. Sharing our Catholic faith made life easier together. Long drives and difficult times gave us many opportunities to pray together.

I was an anxiety queen about financial issues. John frequently wanted us to increase our tithing to our Church, even when money was tight. I would yield to his wishes, and it always worked out that our financial situation would improve soon after. When we once lost a very large account for our business, John said to me, "Do you know what we need? We need to go to Adoration." And we began to try to attend the Adoration of the Blessed Sacrament whenever we could.

In 1994 my dad let us know that his cancer fight was coming to an end. It felt like I stepped onto a carousel and couldn't touch the ground with my feet. After hanging up the phone with my dad, John asked me to come out to the backyard with him.

John had lost his dear mum that year, and he proceeded to give me a blueprint, based on his recent grief experience, of what I could expect to go through when the impending train of my dad's death would run me over. It was helpful to have this conversation with John.

We visited my dad for the last time that New Year's weekend. My dad asked John to join him upstairs, and he let me know that I was not invited.

My dad told John that he would die soon, and he asked John to continue to love me and take good care of me. John assured him that he would do so, and he let my dad know how much he admired him and that we would be praying for his soul every day. My dad and my husband were amazing and very real men. I am blessed.

The Calm Before the Storm

*Our Lady of Mount Carmel parish hall, 2010,
Littleton, Colo.*

John's Fourth Degree Knights of Columbus Ceremony, Nativity of Our Lord Church, Broomfield, Colo., February 2014

The first time I saw John, I saw the kindness of Our Dear Lord in his eyes. I am so grateful to have met and married him. We would have swum through shark infested waters to bring each other a glass of lemonade. We had the kind of marriage that no amount of money could buy, and that no amount of trying could fake. It was the real deal. I am joyful for the way he lived his life, and I wish to continue to try and find the peace that he had found.

A priest we once knew described us as "Nice people, but a couple of characters!" That summed us up pretty well.

Grief

The Moment Our Lives
Changed Forever

Detail of "Cristo Crucificado" by Diego Velazquez

In March of 2014 we began another of our many home improvement projects together, attaching reflective foil insulation to the underside of the roof in the uppermost part of our attic, using a staple gun.

John described the reason for the attic project in an email to a 4th Degree Knights of Columbus leader. "*I won't be able to attend the meeting this month, as I am in the middle of a home project that precludes evening meetings. I'm working in an attic with blown fiberglass insulation, trying to improve airflow and adding a radiant heat barrier, as well as adding some lights to a bedroom below. I am taking Thursday and Friday off work to get as much done before it becomes oppressively warm in the attic, as the outdoor temp heats up. As this phase of my project will be finished later this month, I should be able to attend the meeting next month. God bless, John Lacroix.*"

John made us a special creamed eggs breakfast on Friday morning, March 28, 2014. We had the day off from working in our orthodontic dental lab, and it was day three of our attic insulation home improvement project. We were two-thirds done, and this should have been our last day working in the attic. John knew I was pretty uncomfortable working in that confined area of space, so he worked to organize the project in the way that was most easy to proceed.

We cut the reflective foil insulation in sections, in preparation for attaching the sections to the underside of the roof ceiling in the attic above our upper story loft and master bedroom. I remember laughing and telling stories with John as we cut the foil sections in our bedroom for an hour. We gathered the supplies and tools necessary for the job, and it took another hour for us to get into the attic and to position ourselves in place to safely get to work.

At 10:20 a.m., John was lying on his back in an attic bay. I was at his knees, handing him whatever he needed. We had several support boards placed across the bay underneath him. When John reached just a small amount further into the corner area of the roof to staple the reflective foil insulation into a corner, the support board under his shoulders broke in half, causing a chain reaction failure for the other boards.

In an instant John fell through the attic roof and down the stairwell of our home. He landed 25 feet below onto the three steps in the lower hallway. I watched him fall and I couldn't catch him. As I swung my right arm around to try to catch him, I hit it very hard on a tress and almost broke my arm. This all happened so fast that my brain couldn't process what I had just seen. After a few seconds of shock, I was able to spring into action and rush to help him.

Realizing how far John had fallen, I didn't expect to find him alive when I descended the ladder and the stairways of our three-level home. Yet alive he was. He was moving in and out of consciousness.

The training from the Citizens Police Academy course we had taken a few years earlier at the Lafayette, Colo. Police Department kicked in; I unlocked the front door for the paramedics and grabbed the phone to call 911.

As I turned to look at John, I realized that he couldn't breathe. He was turning blue, and he was trying to pull himself upright with the stair rail. I was quite certain that he had broken his back, and I knew he needed to be able to breathe. The situation was extremely time critical.

I quickly prayed, and then I said, "Honey, I can't move you, but I can roll you."

That was advice that was given to me from above, as the thought was not mine. It was comforting to have a plan for helping him.

I went to John and rolled him gently onto his right side. Nothing happened. I rolled him gently onto his left side. He put his head all the way back, opening his airway, and immediately his chest muscles started moving and he began to breathe again. I could see his chest muscles moving with his breathing. The proper color came back onto his face. John slowly rolled onto his back again. I held his left arm under his armpit, and he held onto my arm in the same way. I tried to comfort him. John's eyes drifted in and out of focus.

I dialed 911 with my right hand. The woman operator stayed on the line with me until I could hear the ambulance siren 10 minutes later. She wanted to hang up then, but I begged her to stay on the phone with me until the paramedics came in. Adrenalin and graces from God allowed me to keep it together while we waited for help to arrive. All I could think of was how to do my best to keep John alive.

Hearing the ambulance siren that day was so surreal. It reminded me of September 11, 2001, a day that John and I had shared, the beautiful weather providing a paradox with the horror unfolding before us on the TV screen. Here was another sunny day that promised goodness. The sound of the siren pierced the warmth of the day and froze my heart.

Eight paramedics and firefighters began to work with John. They brought in a backboard. All of this had happened within the span of 20 minutes at most. I began to have the space to process what had transpired.

I saw that John's legs were not moving. The lead paramedic told me that John's injuries were serious, and that they would do the best they could for him. The inconceivable nature of the situation was beginning to weigh me down.

It was my 'St. Peter sinking in the sea' moment, as reality took over control of my mind. I started to hyperventilate. A paramedic who was standing next to me noticed my breathing and he told me he would get me a brown paper bag from his supplies for me to breathe into.

At that moment, I heard a man's resplendent voice say to me emphatically, "He will live!"

The words were distinct, and they had the beauty of the resonance of a bell. And I felt like a decision had been made. I wasn't sure what that decision meant, but I felt certain that John would live, and that maybe he would live for a long time. I sensed that an infusion of peaceful strength had come into my body, and I calmed right down.

No one else present seemed to have heard the voice that I heard. I now wonder if John had heard those words too. That strength was to last me for about the next three weeks.

I stood up straight and contemplated what to do next. The paramedic went to hand me the brown bag, and I turned down his offer. He looked totally surprised at my transformation. He asked me if I wanted to go in the ambulance with John, and I said, "No, I'll be there all day. I'll bring my car." The paramedic again looked surprised to see my composure and to hear my words.

I followed the ambulance as closely as I could over to Good Samaritan Hospital in Lafayette. At this point the firemen, police, paramedics, emergency staff and I were the only ones in the entire world who knew of John's accident, and I began to think of the others who would soon have to be told.

As I walked across the parking lot, I felt the need to go back to my original place of attachment and security in this world. I asked my deceased Mom and Dad to come and be with me, as I knew things were going to be very rough. I sensed the spiritual presence of my dad on my left and my mom on my right as I entered the Emergency Room entrance.

John's Last Week

Good Samaritan Hospital, Lafayette, Colo.

There was a flurry of activity around John in the trauma room. An angel named Liena, a hospital chaplain with a soft gentle Latvian voice, appeared at my right side and attached herself to me for hours. She got me a phone, as my cell phone refused to work, and handed me a cup of water, which I proceeded to spill and drop numerous times.

I called Our Lady of Mount Carmel Church in Littleton and asked for our pastor to come to the hospital. Father dropped everything he was doing and headed up to Lafayette. Our son left his workplace in Nebraska to drive home and gather his family to come be with us. I thought a great deal about what that long difficult drive would be like, and my heart ached for him.

They took John up to the x-ray unit to get a full body scan picture. Shortly after he was returned to the trauma room a female doctor came out to talk to me. With Father on my left and Liena on my right, the doctor told me that John had broken his back, and that his spinal cord was completely severed. He would never walk again. John had broken all his ribs, punctured both lungs, and there was significant internal bleeding.

It felt as though my feet had come off the ground and I was on a carousel, spinning around. It seemed surreal, and I could feel that I had a totally blank expression on my face. I was numb, and I called upon Our Dear Lord to sustain me. John was alive, and that was all that mattered to me. He and I would face whatever we had to face together.

Father asked the doctor if he could give the Sacrament of Anointing to John in the trauma room. Permission was granted. The three of us moved into a corner while Father did his best to anoint John during the chaos of the movement of the staff, who were frantically trying to stabilize John's condition and to save his life.

When administering the Anointing of the Sick, the priest recites the sacrament's prayers and blesses the recipient with Chrism oil, which is blessed. Blessings are given on: the forehead – for whatever you have thought; the eyes – for whatever you have seen; the ears – for whatever you have heard; the hands – for whatever you have touched; and the feet – for wherever you have walked.

The beautiful sound of the prayers in Latin helped to calm the chaos, and several of the trauma staff paused to take in the words. I could see that John was listening to Father, and I knew that the Sacrament would bring peace to his mind and would help to calm his fears. It was particularly touching for me to see Father anoint John's feet, given the specifics of John's injuries. This is a reparatory devotion in the Catholic Church.

John's Mom had attended Catholic Mass on nine consecutive First Fridays as a child. It had been many years since she had been able to attend Mass in 1994 when she was diagnosed with terminal cancer. True to the promises attached to those who at some point attend Mass for nine consecutive First Fridays, a priest was available during the last weeks of her life to give her the Sacraments of Penance, Holy Communion, Anointing of the Sick, and to give her Viaticum, her last reception of Holy Communion before her death.

John had made eight First Friday Masses, but he missed the ninth First Friday to visit with his Mum before she died, so he began attending Mass on First Fridays again until he too completed all nine. When John suffered his tragic fall, a priest was available to anoint him in the hospital and to take care of his spiritual needs so that he could have the opportunity to attain a holy death.

After the Anointing, we were told that they would move John upstairs to the ICU. I had called several friends and had been able to reach a close lady friend, who quickly made arrangements for her many children and came to be by my side for five hours that day. To have someone close by with you in your darkest hours is truly a blessing beyond measure.

My friend and I moved up to the waiting room in the ICU. From noon until 5 p.m. they worked intensely on John, trying to stabilize his condition and save his life.

I tried to sneak into the room several times - only to be shooed out by the doctor, who never left John's side. I gave my friend a list of friends who didn't have e-mail to call. The hours of waiting were extremely difficult.

At 5 p.m. I got to see John. He was really struggling, and even though he recognized me, he was highly sedated. It was time for me to meet with the doctor to give him a complete medical history for John. I was glad to have my close friend with me, as after I had answered the doctor's medical history questions, he gave me an extremely pessimistic account of John's situation.

He said that John had three potentially fatal issues; major body system shock from the spinal cord injury, extremely low blood pressure and excessive internal bleeding. Finding a way to balance the low blood pressure and the internal bleeding was very difficult for them. John had a possible bruised heart, and he had broken all his ribs, some ribs in multiple places. There was also a possibility that John would lose the use of his arms and become a quadriplegic.

The word "quadriplegic" particularly stunned me. I decided to keep that possible scenario to myself for the near future, as it was too overwhelming to think about. My friend helped me to find and walk like a zombie to my car, and then she left for home. I headed home knowing that I would have to clean up the house from John's fall before the kids and grandkids arrived. I called a friend, John's best man at our wedding, to come and help me.

We cleaned up the attic debris and everything else necessary to make the house presentable. This cleaning was an act of charity that our friend did for John so that our kids and grandkids would not have to view the mess, and it was very much appreciated by me.

Our family arrived for a very emotional discussion, and another close lady friend also came to offer her help. Her hospitalized husband had generously told her to come to me, as I would need her more than he would that evening.

We all headed back to the hospital at 8 p.m. I held to the back of the crowd, as I was very trepidatious of what John's condition would be.

To my major surprise, John was very alert. His hands were tied to the bed so that he could not pull out his breathing tube, and they had his hands covered with the bed sheet. But he kept raising his hands to let me know that he wanted to hold my hand.

He had a firm grip, and he tried to communicate with us around the difficulty of talking with the breathing tube in place. He smiled at all of us, and his eyes lit up. He was sweet to everyone, and he was very happy to see us. He remained in this mode for an entire week. The only explanation I have for this positive change in his condition was that the prayers of a literal army of people had begun during that day and that God had heard our prayers.

John soon became tired, and we left him for the evening. While my friend was driving me home, she asked when I had last eaten, which was breakfast, so she took me to Wendy's for dinner and let me know that she would be spending the night with me.

Her presence in the house was a blessing, as the entire night in bed I relived seeing John fall right in front of me and I didn't seem to be trying to stop his fall. Every five minutes I shuttered in pain from this image. I wished I could have fallen in his place. I tried to catch John in my mind and with my body.

I was exhausted beyond any point I had ever reached in my life before.

Early the next morning I told my friend of my trauma. When I went to take a shower, I discovered that my right arm was bruised from the elbow to the shoulder, and then I remembered that I had tried to stop John's fall. My right arm had hit an attic tress when I had swung it towards John to try and catch him, and I had almost broken my arm in the process. I was never so happy to see a bruise in my entire life.

That morning my friend helped me to set up a CaringBridge page for John on the internet and to choose a picture of us for the page. A CaringBridge web page is an excellent way to help loved ones communicate with everyone during a medical crisis. I chose the picture of John becoming a Fourth Degree Knight of Columbus, and the picture also included me and a top-ranking Knight who had knighted John that February day just a few weeks before.

It was one of the highlights of John's life to become a Fourth Degree Knight of Columbus. John was a Knight for almost 25 years. On pancake breakfast Sundays, we would get up at o'dark early and drive to Littleton to set up for the breakfast. He would clean the kitchen before starting the cooking. He ran a tight ship in the kitchen, and you had to be on your toes and working hard to make the grade.

The day after John's fall I arrived back at the hospital at 10 a.m. on that Saturday. John had been asking for me since 7:30 a.m. and had written "Wife?" on a clipboard paper.

That clipboard became his main communication link, as he couldn't speak because of the breathing tube in his throat. It was hard for him to manage to write, and he wrote right-handed instead of his usual left-hand and in a single vertical column from top to bottom. He wrote some of his letters backwards. It gave him such happiness to be able to communicate in that way.

I let John know that I was happy to be able to spend the entire day with him, and that there was no other place in the world I would rather be than with him. He smiled.

On the way to the hospital that morning I had prayed to God the Holy Ghost to give me the words to say to John to comfort him and to dispel his worries and fears. I had no idea what to say to John. I was hoping to keep our dental lab open, but I wasn't sure if I could do so.

After letting John know that I was happy to be there with him, I heard myself say, "I'm keeping the lab open!" I was amazed I had said that. Then I told John that I would have a dental technician friend of ours come and make sure I was fully trained to do everything in the lab.

Words came out of my mouth that I would never have thought of on my own. God was helping me to know what to say to John at this important moment. John gave me two thumbs up for both proclamations, accompanied by a huge smile.

Obviously, these were the words John so needed to hear, and I was touched that John so wanted to make sure that I would be okay, and that I would be able to help pull us through this situation.

I didn't realize it then, but I was helping John to transition into his new life. John's best assets at this time were his faith in God, and me. He clung to his faith, and he clung to my hand.

John's hospital bed in the ICU tilted from side to side at 5-minute intervals so that the skin on his legs and backside would not receive bed sores. I pulled up a chair and held hands with him. As the bed rose and fell, I kept a hold of his sweet hand.

Visitors began to arrive. Dear friends of ours came and held his hand and spoke with him. John smiled and tried to communicate with each of them. He was quite mentally there, and although he was dealing with heavy medications, his kind personality was evident.

The ICU nurses worked on keeping track of all his vital signs around the clock, with each nurse working a 12-hour shift. In the ICU, patients are given time so that their bodies can heal themselves. The nurses are there to do their best to help this process along. Their dedication was inspiring.

John's brother arrived from Canada that evening, and his presence proved to be a blessing to us. He stayed with me and stood by me through the most difficult of the moments to come. Other family members began making plans for their journey to Colorado.

It was at some point on this Saturday that I realized just how courageous and inspiring John's reaction to his injuries was.

I was watching "faith in action.". While going through the normal difficulties of recovering from the severe shock to his entire body, such as tremors, spasms, large fluctuations in his vital signs, etc., he was still smiling, concerned about others, giving everyone a firm handshake, happy to see visitors, thanking the nurses and doctors and trying to stay positive. He was the man that I always knew that he was, even during the most difficult trial of his life. The hospital staff soon recognized his upbeat attitude, and they gave him special care because of it.

I felt like I had a front row seat to something extraordinary. I would look at John in the hospital bed, tubes going everywhere, vital sign machines working away, the bed slowly moving from side to side, etc., and the features that would stand out the most to me would be his frequent attempt to smile around his breathing tube, and the joy and peace that would shine out from his eyes. It was a joyful and sorrowful paradox of an image.

On this Saturday while looking at the peace and joy issuing forth from John's face while he laid amongst a vast array of medical machines and equipment, I heard a man's voice tell me that I would write a book about our journey. I argued with the voice and said that I was not an author. Again, I heard that I would write a book about this.

When I heard those words a second time, I knew in my heart that Our Dear Lord was blessing me with a petition, and that I would somehow find a way to accomplish what He was asking of me.

The best way for me to describe how I felt John was handling this terrible situation is to include here the actions of General Theodore Roosevelt Jr. during the invasion of Utah Beach in D-Day, June 6, 1944.

I'll quote from "War History On-line" – "Utah Beach 75 years ago": *History would prove Roosevelt correct as the landing craft had drifted approximately a mile south before hitting the beach. As one of the first men off his craft, General Roosevelt was able to assess the situation and coordinate the impromptu assault. He was quoted as saying to his battalion commanders, "We'll start the war from right here!" General Roosevelt had a lot to prove about his bravery, being the son of the famous Teddy Roosevelt, hero the Battle of San Juan Hill in the Spanish-American war. He had planned his assault on the Germans at a specific place, only to have his plans reconfigured by the sea.*

I remember that most of the times in my life with John, our landing craft had drifted at least a mile south, something that frequently happens for all of us. And John was usually able to "assess the situation and coordinate the impromptu assault." His response to his accident as he became aware of his serious situation was no different. And as usual, he was figuring me into his impromptu assault. John seemed to always have an ability to "adapt, innovate and overcome." He was just doing now what he had always done in difficult situations.

My mind drifted to some of my earliest memories of my husband. John appreciated the United States military and the sacrifice of their members so that we could stay free. He had nearly served in the U.S. Navy on a nuclear submarine but had been turned down for this service because of failing the physical due to a back issue.

Shortly after we met, we took a road trip to Santa Fe and Taos, New Mexico. In Angel Fire, New Mexico, John pulled into the parking lot of the Vietnam Veterans Peace and Brotherhood Chapel and parked the car. I asked him why we were stopping here. He told me that, unlike him, I was born in this country and that I needed to go into the memorial and see the pictures of the brave men and women who had sacrificed their lives so that we could live in freedom.

Each month the memorial features pictures of 16 soldiers, in remembrance of the battle near Con Thien, South Vietnam, in which 16 men lost their lives. Among the men was David Westphall, son of Victor and Jeanne Westphall, who built the Memorial. Many other pictures of soldiers adorn the walls. Seeing the pictures of young people washing their cars, going to dances, etc., and knowing that they were now gone truly touched my heart forever. And my naturalized American citizen husband was one of the best Americans that I have ever known.

On Sunday of John's week in the hospital there was no way for me to get to Mass at Our Lady of Mount Carmel Church in Littleton. I later found out that our pastor had asked parishioners at all three Masses to kneel and to offer three Hail Marys for John. John had written "Church?" on his clipboard paper. I told him that he was a rock star, and he smiled. When I told him about the three Hail Mary prayers of our parishioners, his eyes teared up in gratitude.

There was a Knights of Columbus pancake breakfast that Sunday morning, and there was a lot of talk about what could be done to help John and me with our situation. People were preparing to do many extraordinary things for us. John and I had always tried to help others. It was very humbling now for us to have to accept the help of so many.

John's brother and I found John very alert that Sunday morning. John wrote "Hire disability lawyer" on his clipboard paper, showing us that he was thinking about our situation and trying to help me with it.

I had a taste of possible difficulties to come on this day when John was trying to ask me what time it was. The wall clock is purposely placed out of the patient's view in ICU rooms. John used head motions and eye movements, all to no avail. It took me 20 minutes to figure out what he was asking, and John was exhausted. He rolled his eyes. I knew I had a lot to learn for the future.

I went back to the hospital that Sunday evening to spend some time alone with John. It was so good just to hold his hand and to be with him. I noticed on the monitors that his vital signs would stabilize and level out whenever I was with him and talking to him. John and I had smiled at each other every time we heard Brahm's Lullaby played over the hospital PA system, as we knew that another precious baby had just been born in the hospital. I said some prayers with him that night and kissed him goodnight on his cheek.

On Monday John's brother and I waited at my home for the arrival of a priest friend of ours from out of town. Father spent a great deal of time talking with me about everything that had happened since John's fall, and gave me some spiritual advice, telling me that John and I were in a way being crucified on the cross together so that many would lift their hearts and minds towards God.

When John first saw Father that day, John wrote "How is your mum?" on his clipboard paper. Father had just returned from a trip to visit his sick mother. We were amazed that John had remembered, and that he was thinking of others instead of himself at this most difficult time of his life.

Father spoke briefly with John in private. Father told me that our spiritual life would be greatly enhanced during this time of extreme suffering. I found that to be true, as the Rosaries that I prayed aloud with John during these hospital days were intense and were felt very deeply by both of us.

On Tuesday the doctors decided to have John lay on his stomach for four hours to see if he could tolerate a four-hour surgery on Thursday to fuse his vertebrae back together. He did all right with the procedure, but I noticed that it wore him out very much. He slept a lot the rest of that day, and although many visitors came, he was unable to visit.

The doctors discussed everything about John's situation with John directly, as they felt, and I concurred, that he was able to make his own decisions, which was amazing.

This Tuesday they had told John about his paralysis. John wrote to me on his clipboard, "I may never walk again." He looked into my eyes. I said, "You're not getting rid of me, you know." He smiled and wrote, "Whatever?" And I said, "Whatever."

There was no question in either of our minds that the other would not be there for us. If I were lying in that hospital bed, John would of course have been there for me, no questions asked.

I have kept all of John's hospital clipboard writings, and I had them laminated. Only a few pages were accidentally thrown out by the hospital staff. John was able to communicate in so many ways besides talking, by using his eyes, eyebrows, shoulders, arms, and hands.

I could see that John was thinking over his paralysis situation. It's one thing to have your spouse totally on board with you. It's another thing to contemplate the rest of your life in this state, as paralysis is a very personal thing.

I learned later that around 80 percent of spouses walk away from an extremely difficult medical condition involving their spouses. John and I both knew that the idea of abandonment would never ever cross our minds. It was golden for us not to entertain this option. We both had each other covered. No matter what. Never leave your partner behind.

I went out to dinner with John's siblings that evening, and when they noticed that I was very distracted, they were patient with me. I missed John's presence so much, and I realized that I had not taken an active role in discussing John's future with the medical staff. I resolved to fully engage with the doctors on Wednesday.

I went alone to see John that evening, and he was groggy, but he still had a beautiful smile for me. We held hands while I prayed a Rosary with him, and he listened and dozed. I so wanted to hold him, and that was impossible, so I took quite a while to weave my right arm through the tubes across his body and my left arm under the tubes behind his head. And the hug that we had was an enormous gift to me. One of the best hugs I've ever had, and I think he enjoyed that hug too.

John grew spiritually in a very large way during that time in the hospital. He had always told me that "It's all about Heaven." At this time, he showed me that he really believed it. He had such a look of peace in the midst of his sufferings. Our son said that he heard a doctor say about John, "I've never seen someone so broken and yet so alive.".

John raised my spirits, not the other way around. The nurses really took to him, and at times they almost seemed to be petting him. It was very touching to see.

I agonized when seeing John suffer so much. It reminded me of Mary, watching her son Jesus being crucified in Mel Gibson's "*The Passion of the Christ*". Mary digs her hands into the dirt many times over, being powerless to stop what she is watching. I felt that it was a blessing to be able to share, in such an infinitesimal way, what Mary had experienced on that agonizing day.

It wasn't John's sufferings; it was the way John held himself that was the lesson for me. John's demeanor, his patience, his gratitude, his friendliness, his thoughtfulness, his acceptance, his consideration for me and others, his forgiveness, his peace.

On Wednesday I connected with the ICU nurse and asked to speak to the doctors about John's treatment plans.

The ICU nurse coordinator told me that they were just waiting for me to ask, as they had been giving me time to spend with John and to focus completely on him.

The medical staff were very informative, and they let me know that they had conferenced together with the trauma surgeons, and they had decided not to operate to fuse John's 20 broken ribs.

Instead, they would operate to fuse John's vertebrae back together so that he would eventually be able to sit up in a chair. John was paralyzed from the mid-chest area down. The surgery to fuse the vertebrae would be a routine 4-hour operation, not without risks, as every broken bone increases the risk of blood clots, but most likely successful.

John would then be sent to a long-term acute care (LTAC) hospital. After a lengthy stay there, he would probably be transferred to Craig Hospital. Craig Hospital is a world-renowned Rehabilitation Hospital in Englewood, Colo. which specializes in spinal cord injury and traumatic brain injury. A patient must be able to tolerate eight hours of physical therapy each day to be admitted to Craig. They gave me a list of LTACs to call to see if they accepted our health insurance plan. I also called Craig Hospital and set up a tour there for our family. The representative at Craig Hospital was very understanding, and she said that she would discuss John's situation at their staff meeting that day.

On this day a doctor gave some of us family members a 3D virtual tour of John's x-rays. As I held my sister-in-law's hand, I felt like my feet had come off the ground and that I was on a carousel again.

John's body was a complete mess. I could see the x-rays and then turn to look at him in his hospital bed through the doorway. His demeanor and optimism did not match his circumstances or what I was seeing in the x-rays. Only his deep faith in God could help me to explain why he was in such peace. John was living in the present, in the very moment, and that is something that I have had to learn to do ever since.

One thing that really stood out in the difficulties that John was facing was his inability to talk. He was a very verbal man, and although he was communicating with us using his eyes, eyebrows, ears, head, and shoulders in creative ways, having the breathing tube down his throat was a true cross for him.

The doctors explained to us that they were postponing performing a tracheotomy on John until after his surgery. Then they could see if his chest muscles would allow him to breathe on his own or if he would need a temporary or a permanent tracheotomy.

John wrote, "Trach?" many times on his clipboard paper, and then he would look at me with woeful eyes. All I could do was to reassure him that relief would come soon.

John was very tired on Wednesday afternoon, and he asked to be sedated and to have no visitors. I stayed with him while he slept.

Later that evening he was in a thoughtful mood, and I noticed that he was moving into a spiritual detachment, a peaceful state of calmness and a non-involvement with trivial matters or exhausting situations. He was at peace with God and with everyone, and he was joyful and sweet. He seemed to be between two worlds, knowing that he would have a difficult journey here and accepting the task, but knowing too that he also would be okay if God took him home soon. The smile on his face was truly lovely to see. He looked fey, displaying an otherworldly quality, as if he had already taken part in experiencing the unconditional love of the next world.

A neighbor later related to me that they felt John was "getting his ducks in a row to be a paraplegic." That totally resonated with me. And I also sensed that John was getting his ducks in a row to make his peace with God and to prepare to die. Now that he had determined that his family would be okay, he seemed to be free to accept both scenarios.

It was through the hard work John did the last week of his life, to forgive and to be forgiven, that he achieved a state of equal balance between trying to accept 'door number one,' death, and 'door number two,' life as a paraplegic.

Witnessing the beauty of his spiritual state and the agony of his physical state was life-changing for me during that extraordinary week. Jesus had taught us how to live, how to die, how to suffer and how to love. By uniting his suffering with the Passion of Jesus, John was obtaining a purpose and a meaning to his very difficult journey.

This moment in time reminded me of a quote from Thucydides: *"The brave are simply those with the clearest vision of what is before them – glory and danger alike, and notwithstanding, go out to meet it."*

I felt that John had gratitude towards me for helping him to save his life after his fall. This gave John the time he needed to put his spiritual, emotional, mental, and physical affairs in order. John had told me many times that he didn't want a sudden death. He wanted an illness or a time of preparation before his death so that he could make his peace with God and be ready for his transition into the next world.

That Wednesday evening John and I talked about the risks of the surgery, and we were both feeling quite certain that he would survive the surgery, as it was a routine procedure to fuse together his vertebrae and to enable him to sit up. We talked about Craig Hospital and the tour that I had arranged for the family to take. He was able to see a few visitors that evening. I left him early so that he could get some rest for the big day tomorrow. My post to CaringBridge that evening was a request to storm heaven for the success of the surgery, and to pray for the main surgeon, whom I mentioned by name.

Life is Not Ended, Just Changed

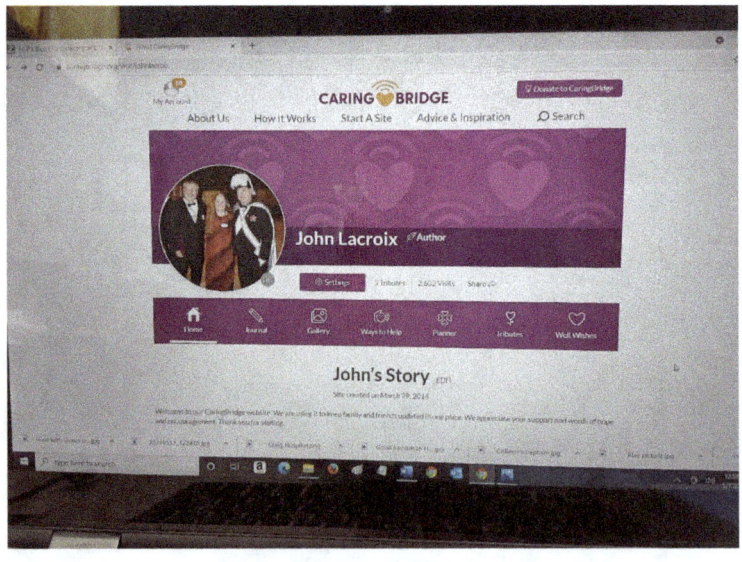

John's caringbridge.org web page

On Thursday, April 3 I woke up early and said some prayers. John's brother and I picked up John's sister and we headed to the hospital. John's surgery was scheduled for 10:45 a.m.

After signing the paperwork for the surgery, I was briefed along with John by the main surgeon about the risks of the surgery. There was concern about John's low blood pressure and the fact that he now had pneumonia. The prior surgery was running overtime, so we waited until noon for John to be taken to the operating room.

John's brother and sister and I spent time with John, and then they left me to have some time alone with him. John had the same spiritual detachment and look of peace and joy on his face that I had seen the prior evening. We spoke very little and just held hands. I prayed with him, and told him encouraging things. I expressed my love for him and told him that we would go through all this together, no matter what.

Finally, the team assembled around John to take him to surgery. As they wheeled him away, I called out "Bye sweetie, I'll see you soon." John smiled at me from around his breathing tube, raised his eyebrows, bobbed his head, and waved at me with all his fingers. John had peace, peace that he had never known before. I saw that peace, and I wanted that peace too. I've never been the same ever since.

I told the staff that I would go home during the surgery. Being only five minutes away, I felt that I could pray the Rosary much better in our home. I told them to call me when the good news came in that the surgery was successful, and we left. We all said very little during the drive home, as we were deeply concerned and apprehensive, and yet we were optimistic that John would be okay. I remember feeling as if my feet were not touching the ground and that I was on a carousel again.

I got comfortable in a wingback chair and prayed a very spiritual and heart-felt series of Rosaries. At 2:30 p.m. our son called, and we both expressed gladness that much time had passed and that all seemed well. I hung up and the phone rang immediately.

It was the operating room nurse. She said, "Did you leave the facility? He's in CPR."

At that moment I seemed to know that John was gone, as I felt his spirit pass by me.

John's brother and I returned quickly to the hospital. I don't know how I was able to drive there.

We ran to the ICU ward, and when they asked me to come to the consulting room, I knew that John had died.

I said, "Oh God, please help me."

They sat me in a chair, and the main surgeon came to me and said that they were still trying to revive John, but there was a good chance that he had gone home to be with Our Lord. The doctor said that he'd be back in a few minutes. I cried very much, and then a calm came over me.

When the doctor came back, an amazing thing happened. He knelt and took my hands in his and placed his head on my knee. He told me that he was sorry. I felt an overpowering desire to console him, and I did. I looked up and saw 30 or so people, probably the entire operating team from the surgery, lined up to see me. They came to me one by one, and I consoled all of them. Some of the ICU nurses who had assisted John during the week but who were off duty that day were called, and they came to see me too. And I continued to console everyone else for many weeks to come.

Family members were called and soon began to gather in John's ICU room. The main surgeon asked if the hospital could order an autopsy for John, so that they could know for certain what had happened in the surgery. The doctor strongly believed that a blood clot had gone to John's heart and caused it to stop, and he wanted to be sure. The surgery had been a success, all of John's vital signs were great, and they were closing the incision in his back when his heart had stopped. We talked it over, and I signed the papers to authorize the autopsy.

The grandchildren were now allowed to come into John's ICU room. John's other sister was to arrive at the airport, and family members left to go and pick her up. They brought John's body into the ICU room. Our grandchildren were moved to the waiting room before he came.

Liena, the angel chaplain, appeared at my right side again, just as she had appeared at the beginning of this journey last Friday. We were so blessed to have John's case assigned to Liena Asupkrapsa.

In her book, "*God's Love Affair – The Heart of Lent*", Liena writes, "*Interruptions are the norm in a chaplain's life. Daily I have the privilege of being called to carry a stranger's cross with them. When the pager goes off, there is no way of knowing who and what tragedy I will encounter. The truth is that I need the crosses I carry with my patients for my own sanctification as much as Simon needs the cross of Jesus for his own redemption. The crosses I carry with others give meaning and significance to my life. They grow in me the fruit of patience and compassion; they encourage me to eagerly seek the face of Christ in every encounter.*"

Father arrived to say the Prayers for the Dead with us. Father said the prayers while I said the responses. I remembered saying these same responses while John had said the Prayers for the Dead over my dad's body in 1995. I stroked John's hair and held his hands. He looked so much more at peace without all the tubes and medical devices. After the prayers were finished, I told Father that time goes by so very fast, and it wouldn't be that long before it was my time to go and then I would get to see John again. Father agreed with me.

I was left alone with John's body for a long while. I so wished that I could go through the door that John had just gone through. It was as if I was sensing the "low door in the wall" from Evelyn Waugh's "*Brideshead Revisited*" that John had just passed through and that I could not access, and I was keenly feeling the separation. I asked God to let me follow John right then, as John and I always did everything together.

And God told my heart that I couldn't go through that door yet. I began to argue intensely with God. I told him that He had made a mistake. The mistake was not that John was dead, but that I was still left here. It was "Inconceivable!", a quote from the movie *"The Princess Bride"*, to me that I was still here, and that I would have to live here without John. I said to God, "Strike me dead, take me now!", a quote from the mother of St. Joseph of Cupertino in the movie *"The Reluctant Saint"*.

And I meant it! I offered point after point as to why it would be all right for God to take me home now too. I wondered if God was playing the "password game" with me, knowing that I so wanted to pass through the door John has just gone through, and blocking me because I didn't know the "password." Maybe on the day I die I will finally know the "password." It was like getting John to the gate at the airport and not being able to go beyond that point with him. I was left at the gate.

While my arguments were heartfelt and had merit, I lost the case to silence. Eventually a nurse let me know that I would need to leave soon. It was a strange feeling for John's brother and me as we left the hospital, realizing that our dear one was truly gone, and that he was not alive in that ICU room anymore.

Shortly after I arrived home I received a call from the Boulder County coroner. He explained that whenever someone dies in a hospital, the coroner must investigate the death. He asked if I was satisfied with the doctors and the hospital, and I said yes. John had received excellent care at Good Samaritan Hospital. He asked me to explain how the accident had occurred, and then he told me that they would issue a pending death certificate and wait for the autopsy results before issuing a final certificate.

I composed a very sad email about John's death and posted it to the CaringBridge site. It was extremely hard for me to hit the "send" button, as I knew my email would break many hearts, and I cried very much. I knew that a large number of people would hold us up with their prayers, and they would help to usher John's soul into Purgatory or Heaven with their prayers.

John's sister arrived from the airport, and my heart went out to her, as she had missed getting to see John alive. The family gathered, and the grandchildren played together.

One granddaughter asked, "Grandma, what are you going to do with Grandpa's clothes?" I replied, "Nothing." And she said, "Oh, that's good."

I spoke on the phone to many people that tearful night. But the phone call I remember the most was from a priest friend, who called very late. I could tell that he had prayed very much before calling, as he knew just what to say. He spoke of John, and of Heaven, and of what is most important; our love of God. His closing words, which gave me much comfort, were "Madam, think of Heaven." His thoughtful phone call gave me the ability to sleep that night.

A Requiem Mass to Remember

John's funeral, Our Lady of Mount Carmel Church, Littleton, Colo., April 2014

On Friday at 8 a.m., John's brother and I arrived at Drinkwine mortuary, which is located directly across the parking lot from our Church in Littleton.

We began the long process of making funeral arrangements for John. Decisions were easy to make as John and I had held many discussions about our last wishes. The main hold up in the arrangements was the autopsy, which was not going to be able to take place until sometime the following week. It would make a tight schedule even tighter since the funeral had to take place on Saturday in order to accommodate the family members from Canada and the eastern United States.

Since the obstacles to having the autopsy take place seemed insurmountable, I prayed and made the decision to be at peace with the outcome of John's surgery and to cancel the autopsy. We all felt relief from that decision, and I asked the hospital staff to release John's body to the Mortuary workers. I gave the mortuary staff the tuxedo that John had worn when he became a Fourth Degree Knight of Columbus in February to use for his burial clothes.

John's brother and I then headed to Mount Olivet to make burial arrangements for John. Once there, I called our assistant priest and asked if he would preside over the burial service on Tuesday. Father agreed, and that gave me much peace, as I knew that would have pleased John. The lady at Mount Olivet asked me what John's last address was, and I was unprepared to think of our home as being his former address. I broke down, and she very kindly helped me through the rest of the process. We followed her in our car out to see John's cemetery plot, which is in the newest far west section, close to a lake and where the mountains are clearly visible.

We arrived at home totally exhausted, and I posted an email to CaringBridge letting everyone know the funeral arrangements and asking church parishioners to bring food to the reception. The CaringBridge web page was a total Godsend throughout this process and many visitors to our page made donations to CaringBridge.

That evening our daughter arranged for a catered dinner at our home for our family and friends. We were all still in shock at the loss of John, and there were many tears and hugs.

My brother was enroute to Denver from Ohio and arrived very late that evening after spending most of the day in various airports due to having missed an early connecting flight. My cousin and her husband drove for over 20 hours straight from Michigan, arriving in the wee hours of Saturday morning. Family and friends cancelled trips, rearranged their schedules, and moved heaven and earth to be able to attend John's funeral on Saturday.

The morning of the funeral, Saturday April 5, arrived.

I drove my brother and brother-in-law down to Our Lady of Mount Carmel Church, and we arrived around 8:30 a.m. People were already bringing food into the parish hall. The hall was nicely set up for the reception, and an area was open to receive John's coffin for viewing.

John's body was brought into the hall at 9 a.m. As they arranged everything for the viewing, the Fourth Degree Knights of Columbus arrived. A young Fourth Degree Knight who had nearly died several years ago from the Swine Flu and severe pneumonia, and who may owe his recovery to the intercession of Cardinal Francois-Xavier Nguyen Van Thuan, told me that he had been very inspired by my husband. I told him that John had been inspired by him and his journey, and that he was the reason why John had decided to become a Fourth Degree Knight.

They placed John's mother's metal crucifix above John's body on the open coffin lid, and his Knights of Columbus sash was laid across his body. I knelt on the kneeler and let my tears fall. They had done a wonderful job in preparing him for the viewing. He looked at peace.

Many came to pay their respects, and then it was time to close the coffin. I knelt to spend one last time with John, and as I looked at him, I wished that I could hold the vision of him in my eyes and in my mind forever and a day.

The church was packed, and the glorious mysteries of the Rosary were led by our assistant priest. Our pastor offered the Requiem Mass in the Latin rite, and he gave a very heartfelt sermon.

My tears flowed, and I was fiercely proud of my husband. The music from the choir was exceptionally beautiful, and I realized that they had offered their talents as a tribute to John's memory. The Fourth Degree Knights of Columbus color guard lent an extra note of respectfulness to the Mass. Our daughter gave me a handkerchief for my tears during the Mass. I soon after used that tear-stained handkerchief to clean the inside of the main altar Tabernacle, a task that I as the current president of the Altar & Rosary Society was honored with once a year on Good Friday before the Mass of the Presanctified.

After the Mass and the placement of John's coffin in the hearse, a line formed, and I consoled many people.

Many healings of old divisions took place and graces flowed, as we realized that day what was truly important in life.

I was summoned into the parish hall, and the Fourth Degree Knights of Columbus presented me with a chalice and paten with John's name engraved at the base, along with certificates of condolence and remembrance. They told me that I could give the chalice to a priest or seminarian, or I could keep the chalice for my family. I was deeply moved.

Hundreds of people lined up to speak with me. No one seemed to know what to say. I usually told them, "There are no words," to which they nodded in agreement.

After the reception I took family members on a tour of our new gothic-style church, the remodel of which had been completed one year prior. John had worked on so many different projects in the church, including the pews and the angel statues near the altar.

He had also given advice and helped to work out logistics for the building of the church. He had figured out where to place all the pews in the church so that a maximum seating number could be achieved. John seemed to be present in every corner.

John's Burial, Mount Olivet Cemetery, Wheat Ridge, Colo., April 2014

On Tuesday, April 7, we gathered at an entrance to Mount Olivet cemetery in Wheat Ridge, Colo.

It was a heartbreaking moment for me when the hearse carrying John's body arrived. I saw the hearse turn the corner and pull into the western entrance to the cemetery.

I said, "My precious baby!"

I couldn't comprehend that John's body was in that hearse, and that we were about to place his body into the earth.

Many folks came on that weekday afternoon. Father said some prayers and two men sang Gregorian chant. I said some words and the family dropped flowers onto the lowered coffin. It was a gorgeous day, and my precious love was now laid to rest in his beloved adopted state of Colorado.

A collection was taken up at my parish to have Masses offered for the repose of John's soul. During the entire month of that June that year a Gregorian set of 30 Masses were offered for John's soul by the Benedictine Priests at the Our Lady of the Annunciation of Clear Creek Monastery in Oklahoma. Shortly afterwards a Novena of nine Masses were offered for me and for our children.

Grief's First Waves

"Le Jour des Morts" by William-Adolphe Bouguereau

I was plunged into a world of total shock. My life had gone from the surrealness of John's accident and the last week of his life in the hospital into the insanity of his death, his funeral, and his burial. The day after the burial, when my girlfriend finally had to go home, thus leaving me alone for the first time since the accident, I had an unsettling moment.

I sat at the dining room table, and I realized that if it weren't for the new drywall repair area on the ceiling below our attic, yet unpainted, and for the plants on the fireplace hearth that were given to me at the funeral, I would have no reason to think any of this had happened. I could fully imagine John walking through the front door. And I would have said to him, "You won't believe the horrible nightmare I just had."

I then fully comprehended that the nightmare really did happen, and that John would not ever be walking through that door again. I struggled to hold it together, and I let myself sit there for a very long time.

I felt like Matt Damon's character in the movie "*The Martian*", which was released that same year. He was left alone on another planet, everything was breaking, all tasks seemed to be impossible to achieve, he couldn't connect with anyone, and no one could connect with him.

I could have starred in a female lead version of the same movie. It was as if the computer of my life had just crashed, and all the data of my life with John was irretrievable, except for the memories in my mind. After spending over three decades of 24/7 contact, conversations and interaction with my beloved partner and spouse, someone had turned the movie off, and I had no way of getting the movie to play again, no matter how much I kicked the TV.

During the week after John's accident, even our home was traumatized. My glasses broke and I had to tape them together and order another pair online. The coffee maker, garage door unit, sprinkler system, dishwasher, and heating system all broke down.

The cats had refused to come back into the house from their outdoor kennel on the evening of the accident, and I had to physically carry them inside. They constantly looked for John whenever anyone arrived, and they slept excessively through most of the first few weeks after John's death.

John's loss tamed me right down. I entered a survival mode as I struggled with crazy things frequently happening. I temporarily lost John's wedding ring. I found my car keys in the freezer. I once forgot where I lived when I went out on an errand.

I struggled with the very concept of whether I wanted to live or not, and of how to carry forward when I didn't want to live anymore. I had loved much and now I hurt much. My five senses dulled to gray and flatlined. I couldn't see beauty, hear harmony, feel texture, smell fragrance or taste flavor.

I felt completely alone in the world, no matter how many loving people I was surrounded by. Hearing myself referred to as a widow for the first time brought a sense of amazement and extreme sadness to me. I dealt with loneliness, sleeplessness, eating problems, geekiness, abandonment, rage, a psych ache of almost unbearable psychological pain, tunnel vision, and a tendency towards isolation or withdrawal. My physical, mental, emotional, and spiritual balances were completely askew. I went through a dark night of the senses and a dark night of the soul. An elephant of grief was crushing me.

And how do you eat an elephant? One bite at a time.

A panic overtook me when I suddenly couldn't remember what John looked like or what his voice sounded like. Friends gave me a large picture of John that Easter. I craved pictures of John, and I saved his voice message greetings to my computer in audio files.

Those early days without John brought out unexpected moments of grief, such as when I did our laundry with John's clothes still in the mix for the last time, and when food he had prepared for us had to be thrown out.

I managed to keep our dental lab open and to adjust to working alone. Sitting in John's work chair for the first time in 30 years was daunting.

I learned the rest of the dental lab skills that John had earlier taught me but had mainly performed himself, thanks to the help of a dental technician friend of ours. He overlooked my awkward mistakes during our training sessions, and he helped me to feel like I could handle becoming the new dental lab owner.

An orthodontist we had worked with for three decades delayed seeing some of his patients for several weeks so that I would have enough time to deliver his work.

Because these two individuals believed in me and in my working skills, I was able to carry forward with the dental lab work.

There were other immediate realities to be dealt with. The paperwork, bills, and legal logistics for the newly bereaved are totally overwhelming. I made huge lists of necessary tasks and worked on whatever items I could handle each day until exhaustion set in and I gave myself permission to go collapse and binge watch some Netflix shows. That to-do list would still be there tomorrow.

One of my worst early moments was my trip to the Boulder County Vital Records office to obtain a certified copy of John's death certificate.

The mortuary had given me the option of going there myself to expedite the certificate process. It was a bad decision on my part to go there. I couldn't find anyone to go with me, and I arrived at the office desk visibly shaking and wearing sunglasses to hide my non-stop tears.

It didn't seem possible to me that John was dead, and here I was asking for a piece of paper to prove it.

A mistake was made by a clerk, and after an extra hour of waiting to complete things, I was able to drive home only after I reached out to a friend on my cell phone.

Our vital record certificates went from being a joyful possession to being very painful to see while

I put certificates together for my meeting with a probate lawyer. Every single account of ours now had to be changed into my name, usually requiring a copy of John's death certificate to complete the changeover. And every single time I had to produce those certificate copies I felt emotional pain.

Something that completely caught me by surprise was that I had temporary "grief cooties." Some people would see me coming, even long-time friends, and I would see them change paths to avoid meeting with me.

I understand now why they needed to stay away from me, as we all deal with grief differently, and many of these folks were dealing with their own feelings about John's loss. I was a constant reminder of his accident and loss. And I'm not sure what I would have said to me shortly after John's death.

The problem with having grief cooties is that you are avoided when you most need human contact, and your feelings of loneliness and abandonment can become intensified. If possible, it's best to greet and smile at someone who is newly bereaved and say either nothing or say something that would be normal words of everyday communication.

Physical problems set in. My stomach muscles became a rock wall for several months until it was determined that I was having an involuntary physical reaction of trying to catch John and to keep him from falling out of the attic. Prayers and breathing properly eventually helped me to unlock and relax those muscles. I became accident-prone, spraining my ankle and falling to the ground on several occasions.

Physical grief frequently manifests itself in lower back pain, respiratory difficulties, and foot pain, along with pain in just about every part of your body.

Grief attacks hit at the most inconvenient times and places, and you have no control over your tears or of what memory or event brought them on. Panic attacks are common. You can lose the ability to commit to meeting with folks and to follow through with that meeting. Trauma from accidents and losses can bring on a sense of hypervigilance when your nervous system filters information at a rapid rate.

Whenever I heard a siren, or the beginnings of a chaotic medical situation, I would instantly go back to the moment when I saw John fall from the attic.

I struggled with blaming myself for the accident, the what ifs of the situation, blocked memories, and a newfound fear of heights. I had to learn to manage my stress better to cope with my trauma symptoms. Prayers and other techniques helped me to work through this hypervigilance.

Making decisions early on was extremely difficult. I put the large decisions on hold for the time being. Attempting to eat out at a restaurant alone was a bridge too far. Learning to deal with other people's schedule instead of being able to do things spontaneously with your spouse was difficult. With a spousal loss you lose someone to do something with and someone to do nothing with.

I remember trying to get my mind around some of the crazy things people said to me.

At John's funeral reception someone said, "Don't worry honey, you're young, you'll find somebody else."

That made me feel suddenly raw and exposed to the world again, after being so happily married to John for many years. Hearing "You need to move on with your new life." made me feel angry about the insinuation that I should be grateful my life with John was over.

Suggestions about how to live the rest of my life came from many diverse sources. I learned to realize that most of this advice was what the advice givers thought they would do if they were in my shoes. And they were not in my shoes.

I began to say to people, "I'm grieving, and all I can do right now is grieve, work, eat and sleep." Tears cleaned the windows of my soul constantly during this time of my early grief journey.

And in all of this, I now realize that I had said some very inappropriate things to folks with a loss before I had experienced my own loss of my spouse.

Early grief is like the movie "*High Noon*", with Gary Cooper and Grace Kelly. You feel abandoned, there is no one to help you when you need it, and you are on your own. However, you do need to do that early part of the grief journey on your own. It is your unique trek back into some sense of reality, and no one else can do it for you.

A sudden loss can add an extra layer of complication to the balancing process, as there was little or no warning of the loss. In her book "*Life Detonated: The True Story of a Widow and a Hijacker*", Kathleen Murray Moran describes very well the difficulties of dealing with a sudden loss.

She wrote on page 61: *It was a strange existence, living a life you were thrust into without choice or preparation. Floating in the ether of indecision, I kept surreptitiously turning to ask Brian's advice, picking up the phone to call him at work, searching for the portal back to the seven years we were happily married... Depression wasn't really the word that captured how I felt. It was more like a complete shutdown; there was nothing left, no escape, no beauty, no sound that made a difference, not even the sound of my children's laughter. Outside people came and went, took walks, laughed and cried, but none of that penetrated the darkness that covered my world.*

A friend read a poem to me in my early stages of grief. I can still hear her lovely Irish accented voice saying:

One of us must go, my love,

One of us must stay.

One of us must go, my love,

One of us must stay.

One of us must go, my love. I'm gone. You stay.

Hope

The Firsts

kintsukuroi

(n.) (v. phr.) "to repair with gold"; the art of repairing pottery with gold or silver lacquer and understanding that the piece is more beautiful for having been broken

When reading the following stages of my grief journey, please keep in mind that no two grief journeys are the same and folks who are grieving most likely will move back and forth from one stage to another, or they will completely skip stages. There is no clear linear path that I have discovered during my grief and trauma journey. The stages I am writing about pertain only to my journey.

I learned to "fake it till I made it," hoping to eventually make it.

Sometimes I made it to events, sometimes not. I felt like a traitor the first time I laughed after John's death. I went through "magical thinking," hoping that I could wish my old life back. Triggers of the memories of everything I had done with John the year before his death popped up at every turn. I counted time as "a month since John died," etc. I felt like I was crazy. I had difficulty focusing while driving, cooking, shopping and trying to function. I was operating on automatic pilot, and I was in full survival mode. I could barely tie my shoelaces. Nothing made sense. I felt like I had gone to live on Mars. It was tough to connect with anyone about anything. Very lonely. Very surreal. I began to do unusual things, like forgetting a family member's birthday or forgetting to pick up a friend for an event. Equipment began to break in the lab. I struggled with decisions. I attempted to clean out a row of things under the microwave counter in my kitchen, only to find the spring-form pan John had used to make fruitcake the year before, and I had to stop right there.

Experiencing medical issues is common, and it is difficult to face those issues when your loved one isn't there to be your partner and advocate. Same with receiving good or bad news, since your partner isn't there to celebrate or console you. Our bodies have a cellular memory around the anniversaries, especially during that first year of loss.

Sadness is an activity that takes a lot of energy, and it can be helpful for us to cocoon for restoration. We sometimes feel alone when we are with people. We can experience "cellular exhaustion," feeling "skinless," and having a hypersensitivity towards touch. We struggle to find our new sense of self, our "new normal."

Along came the first anniversaries, holidays, birthdays, Father's Day, and Mother's Day, Christmas. Each first was like a grief wave coming to knock me down again.

As time went by, the waves became more spaced out so that I even had time to stand up again before another wave hit. I like to think of this process as broken glass on a beach that is continuously washed over, until it becomes a very beautiful piece of sea glass.

My first car trouble without John was a flat tire while driving through a construction zone. A patient state trooper escorted me to Wal-Mart after realizing my widow status and my inability to find the spare tire in the back of my car.

My first birthday without John was blessed with a party from caring friends. A lady friend charitably signed a birthday card for me with the words, "Love from John in Heaven."

My first long weekend alone was Memorial Day weekend. I had a panic attack on Saturday when I woke up and realized I had to face three days alone. I called my dear cousin, and then my therapist. It was a chore to get through each minute, and I only found my way through it with much difficulty.

The first anniversary of John's accident was especially rough. I relived the timeline of that difficult week, paying attention to the day of the week instead of the actual date. The accident anniversary was harder for me to deal with than John's death date. The anticipation of the anniversary was worse than that actual anniversary. Our bodies sense the time of the year, the angle of the sun, and various other triggers, and it causes an involuntary response in us. It is the internal clock of grief. It is best not to attempt to do anything major during these times.

After the first anniversary passed, I felt upset that it was longer than a year ago that I did certain things with John. I could not say, "A year ago we went on a trip." It was an uncomfortable feeling.

I flew to Toronto to spend my first wedding anniversary without John with some of his siblings. Everywhere we went I found myself looking for John, as I had never been there without him before. Getting on the plane to come home was difficult, as I hadn't ever returned to Denver from a trip without John being there. I called a close friend and asked her to convince me to get on the plane to return home.

"Grief attacks," a sudden uncontrollable break down of emotion, are extremely inconvenient. I had a meltdown at a T-Mobile store while trying to change our cell phone plan. The staff brought me Kleenex and a chair and moved the other customers to another line. A T-Mobile phone technician stayed on the phone line with me for an hour-and-a-half and moved John's voice message to a safe place for me. I wrote a thank-you letter about him to the President of T-Mobile.

I kept thinking of the movie "Ladyhawke," where the lovers can almost touch each other between the two worlds, only to be separated at sunrise and sunset. Our separation was agonizing to me. The mundane times were perhaps even more difficult to navigate because company is especially hard to find then. We always get so used to being able to just be with our spouse.

Our minds protect us from traumatic memories until we can process them. I began to slowly remember the difficult things of the last week of John's life, like the surreal 3d x-ray of John while he was in the hospital. It took me two years to remember that I had helped John to breathe at the bottom of the stairs. We had saved his life by my action of rolling him on his side and by John's action of throwing his head back to open his airway passage. Such intense memories take time to safely process.

The flatlining of my five senses would have small periods of recovery. The sound of the coffee grinder reminded me of John at 4:30 a.m. most mornings, and the smell of Stetson cologne could bring John right next to me instantaneously. Sitting on the pier at Lake Dillon in the mountains brought color and beauty back into my vision again that first summer.

Travel was completely different without John. Many adjustments had to be made. Going to certain stores and restaurants without John for the first time took much energy and courage. Some of my family and friends did not want to come to my home because of John's accident, and they began to fade out of my life.

When you are overpowered by your grief, the wonderful memories of your loved one become locked up in a vault in your mind. It takes time for those good memories to be released and to become available to you again. Your mind protects all those memories, as at this point you cannot hold both grief and joyful memories at once. You must wait for the grief to diminish. My grief was always there. I could tap into it instantly just by thinking of it.

A neighbor offered to mow my lawn. I made a list of who I could call on for help with various chores.

Something you can do for those who are in the first stage of their grief and trauma journey is to contact them, and offer your specific help, such as food, phone calls, visits, or listening. Folks in this situation are already feeling isolated. When people avoid them because they do not know what to say, it causes those in deep grief to feel even more isolated. There is no need to say the "perfect" thing. Just be there for them.

There was only one thing in my entire life that did not change, receiving Holy Communion at the Catholic Latin Mass.

When it was hard to get out of bed, much less dress nicely and drive for an hour to church, I continued to go as often as I could. I did not feel like walking up the aisle and sitting in the pew we frequented. I knew lots of folks were watching me, knowing my pain, and wishing the best for me. Faith is like stepping off a cliff and not knowing if you will be caught. And every time I attended the Mass, I was so awfully glad that I had come.

The Latin Mass is never changing, always consistent, and ever comforting. I was in a dark tunnel and there was a light at the end of that tunnel. It was not another train coming at me. That light was the light of God, *Lux Dei*. And by receiving Our Dear Lord in Holy Communion, I found the link to come back into my life.

Our pastor had taught us that our suffering became meritorious when we united our suffering to the suffering Our Dear Lord endured in his Most Sorrowful Passion. He also taught us that there is a sweet spot in everyone's soul. Receiving Holy Communion, the Eucharist, touches that sweet spot in my soul every time.

Reconfiguring My Route

Knights of Columbus Council 13205, Our Lady of Mount Carmel Church, Littleton, Colo., painting my deck, August 2018

I decided to face my grief and trauma head on, like driving an 18-wheeler through a brick wall. No drugs, no hypnotism. I knew I would have to go through this terrible ordeal at some point, or the grief would start coming out sideways, perhaps in illness, anger, or depression.

I wanted to do this journey as soon as possible. I hoped to someday reach a state of homeostasis, a state of normalcy in my life, and I didn't want to delay that journey for a later time and risk always living my life looking backwards. I dove into the ocean of grief, and I tried to swim to the other shore of a normal life again as best I could.

It was my extreme good fortune to find an excellent Catholic faith-based one-on-one therapist shortly after John's loss. My first session was spent relating the accident and loss of John. The second session I was already worried about Christmas. Since it was May, my therapist assured me that we would deal with Christmas when it was nearer. I wanted to help others right away. She wanted us to help me first.

Another good move I made early on was to attend a grief support group. The county where I lived was one of only a few that had a sudden loss grief group available, and the fact that sudden loss of a loved one was specifically dealt with made a huge difference for me.

My first meeting was terrifying. I remember that most of us had that "deer in the headlights" look in our eyes, as we were having trouble focusing on this new life, still in shock over what had happened to us so suddenly. It was the strangest feeling for me to try and understand how I had happened to be at this group meeting that evening. The two co-facilitators had experienced a sudden loss many years ago, and to me their eyes looked focused and normal. I began to have hope that my eyes would once again look focused and normal again too.

As the months went by, the members of the sudden loss group began to call each other "The nicest people we never wanted to meet." I can't imagine not knowing them now.

I found a Christian naturopath who provided acupuncture and chiropractic care for me. These treatments were beneficial for helping me with the imbalance of my body, especially my central nervous system, due to the trauma of witnessing John's accident, of all that had ensued in the last week of John's life and in the early months after his loss. The body in grief and/or trauma will do many involuntary things. Getting a massage was also helpful for those aches and pains.

This was the time to develop a support system. I made a list of what I needed to do, and who could possibly help me with those tasks. I included who I could trust, and who I could call at any time of the day or night. There are very few folks who will answer a phone call from you in the middle of the night. They are golden in our lives.

Loving support continued to pour in for me. My neighbors visited me and invited me to their homes. The Knights of Columbus of my parish organized a clean-up day at my home in May, and my yard and home were put in tip top shape.

The connectedness of being in a Church parish was so helpful to me when I went through my loss. Most homeless folks disconnect with family, friends, and community first before they spiral downward into homelessness, drugs, and alcohol. I had the benefit of my enormous parish family when I needed them the most. And they absolutely rose to the occasion to help me.

Among my early supporters were a family who "adopted" me. My close family had moved out of Colorado due to the rising cost of housing. Facing being alone on holidays and other important times, my new family gave me a standing invitation for any of those dates, unless I had other plans. That standing invitation was a Godsend to me. Other friends invited me to come to their family celebrations. Some couples invited me to be with them, even though I was not a couple anymore.

In the months after John's loss, I frequently drove past Good Samaritan Hospital. Many times, I would think, "Where is the operating room where John died?"

I asked officials at the hospital for permission to visit the operating room, and my request was granted. I brought a neighbor and my grief group facilitator with me. We were met by Chaplain Liena and two nurses. They brought me to the actual operating room, and they also brought in an operating table like the one that was used in John's surgery. The table was modified to allow the patient to lay on their stomach for back surgery. We all held hands, and I prayed. I could sense John's soul in the room. It was so good for me to have this visual experience of where John's soul had left his body.

I asked the two nurses if they had been at Good Samaritan in April. One nurse let me know that she had been one of 15 staff members who had been called in to help when John went into cardiac arrest. They had spent 30 minutes trying to revive him. I could see that she was still very emotionally burdened with that experience.

She told me that they were all about saving lives, and they were not able to save John. I told her to look around the operating room, where the finest state-of-the-art equipment was available. If they were not able to save John with all this equipment at their disposal, then I was at peace with their work, and I believed John's soul was at peace too.

I was giving this nurse the peace about John's death that I was still struggling for and hoping to achieve. I was paying it forward. The nurse looked like a huge burden had just rolled off her back.

I asked her to tell the other staff members what I had said. I thought that perhaps I was supposed to be there at that time to tell the nurse what I did. Then we were able to tour the ICU room where John had been and visit the trauma room where John had first been helped after his accident.

It was a healing experience for me. Good Samaritan Hospital had been an emotionally painful place for me up to that point. In my mind the hospital now became a place where they had taken excellent care of John. How they were able to keep him alive for that last week of his life I do not know.

Craig Hospital, Englewood, Colo.

During John's week in the hospital, I planned for our family to tour Craig Hospital in Denver. We all hoped that John would eventually be able to withstand the 8 hours-a- day of physical therapy that Craig Hospital requires for their patients.

A kind administrator at Craig allowed me to come and take that tour three months after John's death. The work they do with paraplegic and quadriplegic patients is inspirational and astonishing. At the end of the tour, she asked me to remind her of John's injuries. She let me know that John would not have lived long. Her statement came as a shock to me. She told me that John's body had been so compromised that a cold could have easily led to pneumonia, and blood clots and strokes would have been a constant danger. She gave me as an example the movie star Christopher Reeve, who after his horse-riding accident was made a quadriplegic. He was able to afford excellent 24/7 care. Christopher lived for several years, and then he succumbed to an infection after many, many struggles to survive.

The headstone for our graves arrived at Mt. Olivet Cemetery. Seeing it for the first time was rough.

In the beginning I needed to take someone with me. Eventually I braved it and went alone. The first time I went alone to John's grave, I spotted a large gang of youths visiting a grave a few rows away from John.

As I got out of my car, I heard one of them say, "What is she doing here?"

There was tension in the air. I took a deep breath and walked up to them. I introduced myself and said that I liked to meet the neighbors and then pointed to my husband's grave.

In an instant we were all on an equal playing field because of the universal bond of loss.

They offered me a beer, and we all walked over to John's grave with their dog. They told me that their friend was only 19 and that he had been shot by a man who was trying to get into a gang when he opened his front door one day. Their friend left a wife and baby, and many friends too. I often pray for this "neighbor's" soul.

I expected my therapy sessions to be all about my grief and trauma from John's accident and loss. I soon realized that my grief therapy gave me an opportunity to deal with many other issues in my life.

In this early stage of my grief and trauma I began to recognize and respect the grief journeys of others who were missing John. Some would completely avoid mentioning John. Others would let me talk about John for hours. Everyone had a different way of handling their grief journey.

A loss is like a mobile, with all the family members and friends hanging on thread in a balance. When one member dies, the balance is thrown off. Relationships change. The roles that the deceased member did have to be reassigned or dropped. It takes time to rebalance the mobile, or to have it not be rebalanced again.

Feeling the distance of time going by without John meant that people were beginning to think about him less. I still wanted to remember him and to talk about him. This also made me realize that someday I will not be here, and the memory of me will also fade from people's memories.

Adjusting to the change of always having to deal with other people's schedules proved difficult. I was not a constant companion to anyone anymore. I would have to rebuild my "prime time" life of weekends and evenings. Most folks, married and single, already have their "prime time" life worked out. I had to completely start all over again with mine. I missed being able to do something with John, or nothing with John. There were no more spur-of-the-moment activities to look forward to.

At this point in my journey, I learned to try to cherish and connect with others, and I learned how to do a whole lot of things that were totally out of my comfort zone. This was also the time when I was able to have my first "belly laugh." The return of a sense of humor is greatly beneficial for our recovery journey.

For those who might be in the reconfiguring route stage of their grief and trauma journey, including them in your plans whenever you can, and treating them as you normally would as if the loss had not occurred can be helpful to them. They will most likely appreciate anything approaching normalcy in their lives.

Balancing and Accepting

Jeans quilt made from John's jeans and shirts, 2016

Rainier Maria Rilke once wrote:

Be patient towards all that is unsolved in your heart and try to love the questions themselves, like locked rooms and like books that are now written in a very foreign tongue. Do not now seek the answers, which cannot be given to you because you would not be able to live with them. And the point is, to live everything. Live the questions now. Perhaps you will then gradually, without noticing it, live along some distant day into the answer.

I continue to try to live my way into the answers.

Balance and acceptance are two goals that we all probably struggle with our entire lives and that we will most likely never completely reach. I am not saying that we should ever fully accept the loss of our loved one as something that is okay. It will never be okay with us. We can maybe try to accept that it did occur and go from there in search of a new balance.

I worked my way into an acceptance that God did not cause the accident. It happened because of John's and my free-will decision to be in the attic working on that project. We were accountable for being in the attic. We were not culpable for the accident. God was not to blame for the accident.

Speaking of balance and accepting, I tend to immediately have an argument with God about any changes that come into my life. I've never won any of those arguments. So far, He's undefeated. I think the score is now one million-plus to zip. I guess I just need to vent when my plans go array and when what I think should happen doesn't occur. Usually after time passes, I can see that those changes have brought about some unexpected good. Admitting that helps with my journey for humility.

People living with losses must deal with rebalancing their lives, while at the same time also dealing with those in their lives who may seem to place a stigma on the circumstances of the loss, such as severe suffering, mental illness, suicide, or fear of losing their own spouses or family members. Since it is not necessary, and maybe even impossible, to change someone else's perception of the loss, a good thing to do is to focus on your task of rebalancing your own life.

A useful technique given to me by my therapist was the HALT method.

Was I hungry, angry, lonely, or tired? What did I need right now to resolve any, or even all four, of those issues in order to regain some balance?

Also, when facing fears, she taught me to say "and then what?

Fear is not as scary as when it is in the light.

For discouraging thoughts, she taught me to say, "Tell the truth to the lies." Is this in my control right now? If not, give it to God, if so, take care of it.

She encouraged me to have a limit on relationships that drained me, and to find more helpful relationships. Her advice to try to always have something to look forward to, and to try and have a backup plan when people cancel plans with you proved invaluable.

She reminded me that we never know someone's full story, so be gentle with them. I tried to learn to forgive people for things they said and did that hurt me, and to realize that they were carrying crosses too, some of them invisible.

And perhaps the most important lesson she taught me was that Catholic mindfulness is living in the present moment. Manna was only given for one day, so why worry about the next day? She would open out one hand and then bring the other hand into the palm of her hand in a chopping motion, reminding me that I needed to be right here right now, not off to the left in the past, or off to the right in the future. She made this motion to me so many times that I began to have dreams of her directing me like a traffic cop. I will always be deeply indebted to the therapist I was able to connect with so early on in my grief journey.

Analogies are a creative way to try and make sense out of the chaos of our losses. One of my analogies was that John and I were two fish swimming in a beautiful stream, only to both be caught; John going somewhere else, and me, in shock, being moved to a new body of water that did not make any sense. When Mount Everest was in my face when I woke up, I tried to push the mountain further back into the landscape of my mind's eye. It was still there, but that made the day seem a bit more manageable.

Making a list of achievements and keeping it updated was extremely beneficial to counter those days when I was feeling very discouraged. It really helped me to see the progress I had made in a short period of time. Doing a spiritual, physical, mental, and emotional "bucket list" can help as well.

I tried to continue some of the traditions that I had done with John, such as reciting the Litany of St. John the Baptist for the intention of our family members on the way to church each Sunday. Washing John's SUV on his birthday felt right, and making his birthday and our anniversary a happy day proved to be a good plan. I put up pictures of John's restoration work in a bathroom as a reminder of how much he loved to work on those types of projects.

Establishing lists of portals of comfort and security that are places to go in person or in your mind that bring you the happiness, comfort, and security of being with your loved one can be helpful. Examples of some of my portals were my home, our church, our favorite restaurants, places we had visited, and the cemetery where John is buried.

Self-care has become a new and important component in my life. This included making my life easier by temporarily hiring a cleaning lady, asking for help with lawn mowing, snow shoveling and whatever tasks I could not handle myself.

A young man from church volunteered to finish building the drawers for the end tables John had been building for us. Our auto mechanics learned of John's death from his obituary and sent me a card signed by all 15 employees. They took great care of my cars for many years afterwards.

I learned to take care of myself in all the ways that John and I would have taken care of each other. And self-care such as putting the oxygen mask on myself first during a crisis helped me to eventually be able to take of others as well.

As part of my self-care habits, I have come to understand that every year from late March to early April my body keeps the score of the events of 2014, and I usually go into an involuntary mode of certain grief reactions during that time. Each year is different, and the reactions have diminished as the years go by. And yet I have learned how to honor what my body needs to do, and I try to go more gently and to make less plans for that week every year.

I remembered that John had a habit of pacing around the room when he was thinking of how to make a major decision, and I decided to start walking 10,000 steps a day each morning. It was like walking the Camino de Santiago Compostela (the Way of St. James, a lengthy hiking pilgrimage in Spain), only in my own home. It became my pilgrimage to God. Hippocrates once said that walking puts the brain into a rhythm. I prayed as I walked, and this regiment became my way of helping myself to try to live the questions of the physical, spiritual, mental, and emotional aspects of John's accident and loss.

I found a way to memorialize John's memory through the work of a woman who makes Memory Bears out of a loved one's clothing. I took John's robe and shirts to her and asked her to make Memory Bears for all the members of our families. The bears were well received. And I made a quilt out of John's shirts and jeans. The diagonal rows of colors make the quilt have a similar appearance to the colors that were in his clothes closet.

Kinetic sand is also beneficial for grief therapy. In the movie "*The Passion of the Christ,*" Jesus' Mother, Our Lady, lets the dirt fall through her hands as she watches her son being crucified. This reminds me of why continuously clutching kinetic sand in your hands is such a great way to help release tension caused by the grief and trauma from your body. Give it a try sometimes. It is rather addictive.

Most of the Mars scenes in 'The Martian' (2015) were actually filmed on Earth

A sense of humor is always a plus during a grief journey, hence this meme. Having felt like I lived on Mars for a while, it seemed like I actually did see some of the filming of this movie there in 2014. Just kidding!

Several movies, besides *The Martian*, (2015), had an impact on me during this phase of my grief journey.

The movie *Collateral Beauty*, 2016, with Will Smith and Kiera Knightley, caused me to make a list of the collateral damage verses the collateral beauty in my life after the loss of John. Collateral beauty is the unexpected moments of charity and beauty that happen after tragedy and loss. These moments would not have happened if the tragedy had not occurred.

The movie *The Impossible*, (2012), with Naomi Watts and Ewan McGregor, about the Indian Ocean earthquake and tsunami of 2004, reminded me of how similar a personal experience of a natural disaster is to the personal experience of a devasting sudden loss of a loved one.

When seeking a support system, choosing people who are more grounded in their own emotions can be helpful. They are more able to hold their space with you while you are extremely broken. It may not be a good idea to be around folks who are emotional-ly unstable themselves.

I began to realize that my loneliness was my responsibility and not anyone else's. I needed to own it and find a balance for it the best I could.

The four groups of connections I tried to work on were my intimate family inner circle, my friends and acquaintances, my community and my relation-ship with myself. Isolation can lead to stress, a fight or flight reaction, physical illness and even auto-immune problems. I often had to step out of my comfort zone to resolve this issue, and it was worth the effort.

The following are some things that people shared with me during this stage.

I told someone, "Someday I'll get through this." And I was told, "Start saying someday is today and I'm good now."

A spiritual friend told me that "we lose our loved ones in pieces".

Someone told me that "feelings buried alive never die."

A member of my grief group told us her husband had always said, "All you need is 10 seconds of courage, and you can do anything." She also told us she used the "bless and release" method when dealing with folks who say inappropriate things to her about her loss.

A priest told me that, "God can give you more than you can carry, ask God for help,"

A family member said to me, "You're doing better than you think you are."

And someone shared that, "Life is a delightful nightmare."

Finding hobbies and work that nourished my soul were beneficial. Grounding activities, such as quilting, walking, and praying helped me to relieve stress.

It was helpful that John and I had discussed the possibility of either of us dying early. This assist-ed me in dealing with his final arrangements and to know that he wanted me to learn to live as fully as I could after his loss. His death caused me to think of my own death, and to wonder what I should do with the time I had left.

J.R.R. Tolkien wrote in *The Fellowship of the Rings:*

"I wish it need not have happened in my time," said Frodo.

"So do I," said Gandalf, "and so do all who live to see such times. But that is not for them to decide. All we have to decide is what to do with the time that is given us."

Our pastor once said in a sermon "God chooses our time of death. He will not hasten it for those who despair. Nor will He delay it for those who are timid. Wisdom comes from meditating on death."

Priorities became clearer. I did not have much time for unimportant things. And I have learned that we do not get to choose to live in the same years that our loved ones live in, so it's good for us to cherish the time that we do have together with them now.

It became apparent that I needed to deal with disposing of some of John's possessions. I attended a workshop given by Rachel Blythe Kodanez, a widow who lost her husband at an early age. Rachel came up with a six-pile theory of how to successfully deal with a loved one's possessions. Her book *Finding Peace, One Piece at a Time* is highly recommended.

I learned that while living life here without John, I did not have to keep everything the same. If John had lived, we would have changed some things. And the reality of a new work and life schedule dictated that living alone now meant some things had to change.

I decided to stay in my home. It became a sacred place, as John and I had worked to save his life at the bottom of the stairs the day of the accident. It was difficult to stay in the same environment at first. My home looked the same, but it was certainly a different place.

Like the change of pace from failure into victory in the music video *The Walk of Life* by Dire Straits, things slowly began to start to make sense again. The sound of the coffee grinder brought back John and his early mornings; the smell of his Stetson cologne brought back his physical presence. After all my five senses had flatlined from my grief, they began to return, and they were now enhanced.

I contemplated making bigger decisions, such as having our wedding rings joined together and made into a necklace. At this point in my grief journey, I had learned to take risks.

For folks who are in the balancing and acceptance stage of grief and trauma it may be helpful to encourage them in their decisions and journeys. It is easy to want to tell them to do what you would do in their situation. Since each situation is unique, they would most likely want to hear that you are supportive and that you are there for them. Be especially kind to folks who appear to be stuck in their grief journey. Charitable behavior from others will more likely than not encourage them to leave 'Mars' and to return to 'Earth' again.

Processing the "Why"/
Survivor Guilt/Dreams

"Hands of An Apostle" by Albrecht Dürer, 1508

Another helpful way to process grief and trauma is to examine the "why" of our losses, the "what ifs" and "if onlys" notions that continue to surface in our thoughts and dreams. Our hearts and our minds will demand to know why this loss happened, and it will be difficult to find our peace of soul again until we allow ourselves to explore what happened in depth. I am a big believer in sifting through these types of thoughts and feelings whenever someone in grief is feeling balanced enough to address them.

There was no possible way that I was to blame for John's accident. And yet it is totally normal that I was plagued by those accusatory thoughts, and that I also struggled with survivor's guilt, the guilt or shame you feel for surviving a traumatic event in which others did not.

I asked myself, "Why am I still here when John is not?"

I felt strongly that I would have wished to have fallen in his place, or to have saved him from his fall. And I kept hearing lies in my mind from dark sources about the accident being my fault.

So sometime in late 2017, I imagined in my mind that I was in the attic where the accident had happened, and I gathered a jury of 12 peers and a judge.

I was the prosecuting attorney and the defense lawyer. I presented the case against myself for being at fault for what had happened to John. I was tough on myself, talking about all the "what ifs" and condemning ideas that had floated around in my mind these past three years.

Some of it was scary for me to think about. Nothing negative was left out. Then the defense presented a story line of events leading up to the accident, including John and my method for doing home improvement projects, our safety concerns and actions, our rhythm of work habits, our years and years of teamwork, and everything that had happened leading up to that tragic moment. Nothing positive was left out.

After some closing arguments, the prosecution and the defense rested. The jury deliberated. A verdict was reached. I was unanimously acquitted of blame for John's accident. The jury also stated that John had no culpability of blame for his accident. The judge dismissed the case.

Had I been convicted of blame for John's accident, I would have happily served whatever sentence of punishment the judge handed down, as I would then finally have felt that I had paid for my crime. Innocent or guilty, eventual peace of mind could be achieved.

What I learned from my imaginary trial by jury; I was not meant to catch John, to keep him from falling or to keep him from sustaining his injuries.

I was meant to be there for him when he fell, call 911, unlock the door for the paramedics, save his life along with him by helping him to breath, make his time in the hospital easier, make his transition into the next world easier, take care of his final arrangements and burial, keep our home and business going, keep his memory alive with family and friends, write a book about us to help others, lead a better life the rest of my life in honor of the way he lived his life, and to learn to be better at listening to God.

As a side note, a priest once said, "The evil one is the prosecuting attorney at our particular judgment. Our Lady is our defense attorney."

Another important part of the grief and trauma journey is the dreams we have of our departed loved ones. While I have had many dreams of John, there have been a handful of dreams that I would call "significant."

I can remember these dreams vividly, as if I have just dreamed them. Each of these dreams taught me an important lesson, and they came progressively in time according to my ability to be open to higher levels of the acceptance of John's accident and loss. None of these dreams told me what to do or predicted the future. These dreams guided me along in my journey.

Things I learned from these significant dreams included: seeing John as not broken anymore, learning that I was not to focus on John's physical accident and that all would be provided for me going forward, that love in the next world would be perfected in a way not possible here, that I could talk to John whenever I wished to and he would hear me, and that Our Dear Lord had caught John spiritually not physically at the bottom of the stairs - and therefore I didn't need to continue to try in my mind to catch John or to stop his fall anymore.

Many of our family members and friends have also experienced dreams and visions of John as well. I am often asked why we have received these gifts when others wish so much to have even one dream of their loved one. This is a mystery, and I do not know why we have been so very blessed. My only guess is that perhaps an openness to dreams of our departed loved ones can come from working on our acceptance and balance about their loss.

At this point in my grief and trauma journey I had learned to be vulnerable and to try and be open to new ways of thinking about my grief and trauma journey.

A good thing to do for folks who are in the 'processing the "why" survivor guilt and dreams' stage of grief and trauma is to allow them to safely explore the various issues that frequent their thoughts and dreams when they can.

It would be easy to discourage their journey into uncomfortable places at this time. However, it is sometimes necessary for them to swim in the ocean of uncertainty and uncomfortableness before they can reach peace of mind about the loss of their loved one. Their loss will never be totally acceptable to them. They will want to try and find a way to live with the loss. Let them swim in that ocean if you can.

Growth and Helping Others

This is a reminder about the **Survivors of Sudden Loss Group** meeting this week:

Date: Thursday, August 2nd 6:30-8:00

Location: Boulder (see map/directions below/attached)

Facilitator: ---- ------ & introducing Jodi Lacroix as a new official co-facilitator!!

Email from a Sudden Loss Grief Group in Boulder, Colo., August 2018

Since learning that grief and trauma often go together, I also learned that grief and trauma may require separate recovery journeys. I first focused on the grief journey. Sometime later it became beneficial for me to focus on the post-traumatic stress disorder I had obtained due to witnessing John's accident.

Post-traumatic stress disorder (PTSD) is a mental health condition that can result from either experiencing or witnessing a terrifying event. Symptoms can include uncontrollable thoughts about the event, nightmares, flashbacks, and severe anxiety. Experiencing this condition is not pleasant, and a lot of work is required to overcome the symptoms that happen when triggers of the terrifying event occur.

The day after John's accident a friend told me that whenever in my mind I saw John fall, I should say a prayer.

I began right away to say, "I love you Jesus" every single time I recalled seeing John fall.

This short prayer would always help me to move my thoughts away from the accident and to become calm again. I have said this prayer a countless number of times. This prayer meditation technique was extremely helpful to me.

It takes time and patience to break the triggers and thought patterns of a traumatic experience in your mind. Other treatments for PTSD include cognitive therapy, a talk therapy to help you recognize ways of thinking; exposure therapy, a behavioral therapy to help you safely face the situation and memories; and Eye Movement Desensitization and

Reprocessing (EMDR), a series of guided eye movements to help you process memories and change how you react to them.

EMDR uses eye movements and sometimes rhythmic tapping to change the way a memory is stored in the brain, and this can allow you to process the memory and recover from the effects of the trauma. I took advantage of EMDR therapy to overcome my trauma from John's accident.

I also used it to recover from my trauma of almost dying alone in my home from Covid in March of 2020. For an hour I fought for every breath at one point, and I was very near the point of losing the battle to live, when the virus temporarily released my lungs from its grip. During that hour I begged God for the chance to tell my dear ones that I loved them. For all of you who did lose loved ones to Covid, I'm fairly certain that they were thinking of you in their last moments and wishing to tell you how much they loved you. I hope that this witness from me can help to bring you some comfort when thinking of your loss of them.

While dealing with PTSD, I learned in my grief support group about a positive side to experiencing trauma, something called post-traumatic growth (PTG). I shifted my focus to doing the necessary work to obtain this beneficial goal.

Post-traumatic growth (PTG) is a positive personality change that can happen after traumatic life events are experienced. The theory of PTG was developed by psychologists Richard Tedeschi, PhD, and Lawrence Calhoun, PhD, in the mid-1990s, and holds that people who have experienced trauma may be able to show greater optimism, positive outlooks, satisfaction with social support, and an increase in supportive resources in their lives. Not all people who experience trauma and PTSD in their lives are able to achieve post-traumatic growth.

A quote about obtaining growth from author Cynthia Occelli describes the process well:

For a seed to achieve its greatest expression, it must come completely undone. The shell cracks, its insides come out and everything changes. To someone who does not understand growth, it would look like complete destruction.

The five elements to achieving growth from trauma that Dr.s. Tedeschi and Calhoun explore are education, emotional regulation, disclosure, narrative development, and service.

It was certainly painful for me to try and wrap my mind around John's accident and loss. Education and understanding came along very slowly and with much effort. Working through this process with my Catholic faith as a guide was most beneficial.

It was also so easy for me to think about the people I was not hearing from anymore, failed attempts to fix things, and the world of the unknown that I now lived in. When plagued with those discouraging thoughts, I tried to shift to reading through my list of achievements list one more time, thinking about milestones that I had reached, and contemplating the collateral beauty that had emerged from the difficulties I had faced.

It took me two years to be able to write and articulate that I had helped John to breathe at the bottom of the stairs by rolling him on his side. This memory was protectively blocked from the memories of my mind until I was able to process it. I started writing this book several months after John's accident and then I had to work through many periods of writer's block. Being a member of my sudden loss grief group and being able to openly talk about my struggles proved invaluable during this phase.

I tried to find and maintain interior peace and to not let anyone or anything steal my joy with the lovely things in my current life. I remembered more and more my life with John, and the way John had lived his life. I wanted to carry forward in life again as a tribute to John, being forever inspired by his example, especially by his last week of life on Earth.

My grief started to lift somewhat; my guard came down and I began to let the next things in my life lead to steppingstones for the future.

I called and visited who I wanted to, did thoughtful things for others, and did important things when I thought of them instead of pushing them aside until later or never. Moving out of survivor mode and into life again allowed my five senses to come back into focus again. I learned to rely on my sixth sense, trusting my gut instinct for decision making. I allowed the ghosts of my life to come, welcoming them, being open to the next world, and stepping back into life again. My priorities shifted and I contemplated what I wanted to do with the rest of the time I was given here.

After spending five years as a member of my sudden loss grief support group, I was asked to stay on as a co-facilitator of the group. This was an incredible honor for me. If I could help those in the early stages of their sudden losses to stumble even a little bit less than I did in the beginning of my journey, then I considered my input a success. It was healing for me to listen to their stories and assist in any way I could by sharing appropriate thoughts with them. I stayed active in the various groups I was already in, giving my help in any way that I could manage.

In 2019 I was asked to come back to the Loretto Chapel in Santa Fe, N.M. to fix another area on the underside of the spiral staircase and to restore painted areas on the Stations of the Cross. I also took on restoring and gold leafing the altars at Sacred Heart of Mary Church in Boulder and restoring the 16-foot Crucifix at the Augustine Institute in Greenwood Village.

Spiral Staircase, Loretto Chapel, Santa Fe, N.M., July 2019

In June of 2020 I was asked to assist a young artist couple in completing the renovation of the sanctuary at Our Lady of Mount Carmel Church in Littleton. The artists had designed and fabricated the artwork for the sanctuary in the Gothic style, and the results were stunning. In the five months that I worked alongside them, I painted in the side chapels and other areas of the sanctuary. They taught me stenciling and gold leafing techniques, and it was an honor to learn many skills from them.

I hope that the restoration work I did can be a help in the faith journey of those who look upon it. Mainly I wanted to help others and let them know that you can survive an atomic blast to the heart and yet still want to live.

Our Lady of Mount Carmel Church, Sacred Heart side chapel, Littleton, Colo. October 2020

Our Lady of Mount Carmel Church, Littleton, Colo., March 2021, photo by Tamas Kish

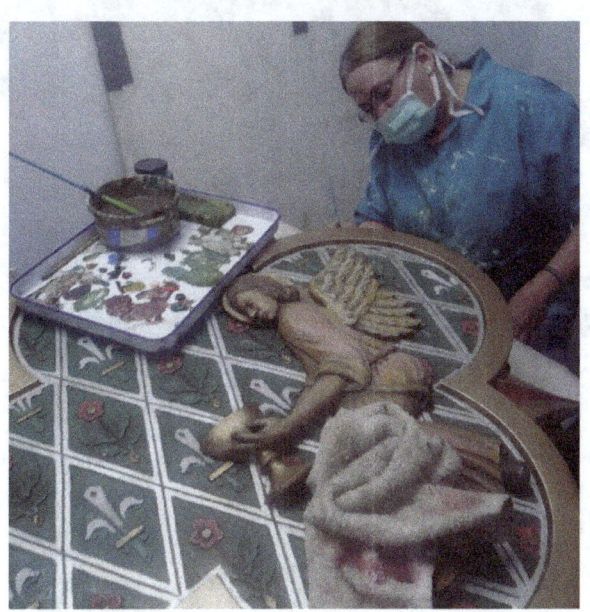

Crucifix for the Augustine Institute, Greenwood Village, Colo., January 2018

Crucifix for the Augustine Institute, Greenwood Village, Colo., January 2018

The benefits of doing the work necessary to achieve post-traumatic growth are legion. I experienced renewed personal strength, found new possibilities in my life, saw some of the relationships in my life improve, became more grateful for the relationships I already had, gained a new appreciation for my life, and enjoyed a deepening of my spiritual faith in God.

A priest once said that true happiness for humans comes from living the virtues, helping others and self-sacrificing. Proof of this came to me one day when I received an anonymous card from fellow parishioners.

They said that they had watched me for several years and they knew that I had suffered greatly. However, they witnessed that I always exuded joy and calm. They thanked me for my concrete and very real example of Christian joy amidst great pain and suffering. They said they loved my smile. This card has brought me great joy. We are not used to being seen on a deeper level, and when we are, it touches our hearts. It is Christ-like, as Jesus sees us.

Interview for the Mass of the Ages movie, Lafayette, Colo., October 2020

In October of 2020 I received the amazing honor of being interviewed for a documentary called *Mass of the Ages*. This three-episode film, which is available on YouTube, explores the richness of the Traditional Latin Mass through stunning cinematography and inspiring stories. Director Cameron O'Hearn decided that the story of John's and my dedication to the Latin Mass over the years, and my commitment to the Mass after John's loss, would be appropriate for inclusion in his documentary.

In the fall of 2019, I attended a party and told the story of John's and my Latin Mass involvement to friends. One friend passed the story along to a family member who was a benefactor for *Mass of the Ages*, and that is how I was 'turned in' to the *Mass of the Ages* (MOTA) crew. When I received a call to be interviewed for the movie, I really did think that a male friend was playing a prank on me, so I enthusiastically said "yes." And I soon found out the seriousness and importance of that fiat.

The MOTA crew of five young men with a van full of professional movie equipment arrived at my home on a Saturday evening. During the interview, Cameron O'Hearn immediately put me at ease, and I felt like we were just having a conversation between each other.

The crew came back early the next morning for more filming, and then we carried the filming of the interview to the Sunday High Mass at Our Lady of Mount Carmel Church, the Carmelite Monastery in Littleton, Romano's restaurant for lunch, the sanctuary at Our Lady of Mount Carmel, and then to John's grave at Mt. Olivet Cemetery in Wheat Ridge.

While we were filming my painting scene in the sanctuary at Our Lady of Mount Carmel, I was told that the Requiem Mass set-up, which is shown at the beginning of *Mass of the Ages: Episode I*, was meant to symbolize John's Requiem Mass.

The way that they were honoring John's memory touched me deeply. The MOTA crew used a camera attached to a drone to film me walking through the cemetery towards John's grave as the sun was setting behind the Rocky Mountains. I made note that during the entire two days of filming Director Cameron was constantly praying and asking for discernment from God as he decided what to film for each scene.

Mass of the Ages crew, Lafayette, Colo., October 2020

Cinematographer Thomas Shannon, filming in the Our Lady of Mount Carmel Church sanctuary, Littleton, Colo., October 2020

MOTA crew filming at Mt. Olivet Cemetery, Wheat Ridge, Colo., October 2020

In August of 2023, the MOTA crew asked me to be filmed for a brief appearance in *Mass of the Ages: Episode III*. During the filming, my two Augustine Institute videographer friends asked me to look up at the OLMC Church ceiling.

This triggered a happy memory for me of John, who had been on the building committee during the construction of our new church in 2012.

John had made me keep my eyes closed until he placed me right where I was now standing. He told me to open my eyes and look up, and I then caught my first glimpse of our beautiful new 40-foot church ceiling.

At that moment of filming the third episode, when I looked up at the ceiling, I saw in my mind my husband and Our Dear Lord, and it seemed that I was being told that I would be with them someday. The authentic joy on my face was captured for my brief appearance in Episode III.

"Mass of the Ages: Episode III", Our Lady of Mount Carmel Church, Littleton, Colo., August 2023

The *Mass of the Ages* movies are iconic, especially to the young generations of Catholics in the world. My hope for the future of the church rests with these emergent faithful; for their zeal, their enthusiasm, and their love for the Latin Mass.

And I pray that John and my story of joy, grief, hope, and of our love for the Latin Mass will inspire others to personally experience for themselves the Mass of the Ages, the immemorial Tridentine Catholic Mass.

As of this writing, disorder has the world in flames. I believe that this form of the Mass will save the world. The Latin Mass is order out of chaos.

At this point in my grief and trauma journey I was learning to heal myself through service and self-sacrifice for others.

A helpful thing to do for folks who are in the 'growth and helping others' stage of grief and trauma is to encourage them in their efforts to take these courageous steps in their new lives.

It is not easy to switch your thoughts and actions into more positive streams and patterns. They may need you to listen, to support and to hold them up during the times that they waver or feel weakened in their resolve to go forward. Remind them of how far they have already come and become their cheerleaders as they learn to focus less on themselves and to focus more on others.

Conclusion

"*Carpe Diem*"
Living Life to the Fullest

Requiem Mass set-up from Mass of the Ages: Episode I, Our Lady of Mount Carmel Church, Littleton, Colo., October 2020

John wanted a hidden life, a small funeral, and to die with five cents in his pocket after giving all his money away. John did not get any of those things.

There is a song by *Mike+the Mechanics* from 1995 called "*Beggar on a Beach of Gold.*" The gist of the lyrics is that we are all unworthy of the beach of gold that God presents to us in our lives, and that it is wonderful to be grateful for that gift.

One day when watching a video of this song, John looked at me with much joy on his face, and he said to me, "I am a beggar on a beach of gold."

I believe he was telling me that he was very happy with the life God had given to him. "As having nothing and possessing all things" Corinthians 6:10.

A priest friend once told me when speaking of John, "He fell into Heaven."

Yes, and maybe with some possible time in Purgatory. In any case I will continue to pray daily for his soul to eventually journey to Heaven, as John once asked me to promise to do.

Since everyone experiences the loss of loved ones at some point in their lives, I'm curious as to why grief therapy is so under emphasized in college level psychology programs.

I'm not a therapist. When co-facilitating grief support groups I call myself a Grief and Trauma Experience Person (GATEP). I'm not a tragic figure; I am a joyful person who has had some sad chapters of life. And I can only hope to be an apostle of encouragement to others.

I can't help bringing more movie quotes into this book.

In the 1943 movie *A Guy Named Joe*, Spencer Tracy plays Pete Sandidge, a WWII pilot, and Irene Dunne plays Dorinda Durston, also a pilot. They are deeply in love, and Pete is killed while on a dangerous mission. Dorinda is despondent. She later commits to marry another pilot, Ted Randall, played by Van Johnson. She vacillates about marrying him because of her love for Pete.

The ending scene shows Pete as an angel talking to her as she flies a dangerous mission.

Pete's last lines to her says it all:

You know the only decent thing I did in my life was to love you. But if the memory of that love is going to make you unhappy all the rest of your life, there must have been something wrong with it. It should have been the kind that filled your heart so full of love that you just had to go out and find someone to give it to. That's the only real kind, isn't it Dorinda? That's that only kind that ever lives.

This movie quote reminds me of the analogy of a heart of glass. After John's loss my heart was broken into a million tiny pieces of glass. And God helped me to put my heart back together again, not as it had once been, yet into a differently shaped heart that is now gentler, and more empathetic and open. I felt able to allow God's love to flow more freely through my heart and then out towards others.

Many who have experienced losses talk about having extra empathy towards other loss sufferers.

Professor Brené Brown explains very well in her Ted Talk on YouTube "Empathy vs. Sympathy," that empathy feels connection and sympathy drives disconnection. Empathy involves thinking about someone's situation through their eyes, trying not to judge them, recognizing their emotions and telling them that you are with them in that basement room and that you will listen to them. Connecting with them is what will make things better for them.

Other grief quotes that made an impact on my journey are from artist Henri Matisse at the end of his life, "The pain passes but the beauty remains." And from *Shadowlands* by C. S. Lewis: "The pain then is part of the happiness now, it's part of the deal," (from his wife Joy to C. S. Lewis), and, "The pain now is part of the happiness then, it's part of the deal." (from C. S. Lewis to his stepson after Joy's death).

Sometimes now I can see the "grief beauty" or the "beautiful agony" in others and in myself; that grieving essence of who we are now as an individual without our loved one here, while at the same time beautifully reflecting out the love that we shared with them from our souls.

It's usually a good idea to take great care in what you say to a grieving person. Listening to them is best. You cannot fix it for them or replace what they have lost. Often you may want them to be back to normal and to quit grieving so that you will not need to worry about them anymore. That is unrealistic. They will always have their loss for the rest of their life. They are now different people than they were before the loss. It will 'take the time it takes' for them to learn to carry the loss forward with them.

If possible, avoid saying: "Don't worry honey, you're young. You'll find someone else" "It's time for you to move on with your new life" "Are you still grieving?" or "It's been so many months (years), aren't you over this yet?"

Some better examples for what you can say are: "There are no adequate words to express my sorrow for your loss. I'm sending you my love and keeping you close to my heart at this time" "You can talk to me about your loved one whenever you want" "You are not going crazy" "I would have liked to have known your loved one" "I miss your loved one too" or "You don't have to talk. I will just sit beside you."

I am convinced that, like the Wedding Feast at Cana story in the New Testament where Jesus surprises the wine stewards by changing the water into the most excellent wine at the end of the nuptial celebration, John and I experienced the best of the wine of our marriage during the last week we spent together in the hospital after John's accident. We were never closer spiritually, physically, mentally, or emotionally. It was the three of us that week, Our Dear Lord, John and me. And it was a beautiful agony.

Go gently, dear mourners. Do things that refresh your soul and try to always keep the list of your accomplishments updated.

I have heard it said that a tragedy goes from joy to grief, and a comedy goes from grief to joy.

May you have the joy of loved ones in your life as you navigate the expected grief. And may you always find hope amidst your grief in Our Dear Lord.

"Pieta" by William-Adolphe Bouguereau, 1876

www.ingramcontent.com/pod-product-compliance
Lightning Source LLC
Chambersburg PA
CBHW071251130626
46556CB00003B/1267